Tipping Point: Transformation and Innovation in the Legal Department

EDITED BY FRANCESCA RAMADAN

Head of events and books
Leah Darbyshire

Commissioning editor
Alex Davies

Editorial assistant
Francesca Ramadan

Published by ARK Group:

UK, Europe and Asia office
5th Floor
10 Whitechapel High Street
London, E1 8QS
United Kingdom
Tel: +44(0) 207 566 5792
publishing@ark-group.com

North America office
4408 N. Rockwood Drive, Suite 150
Peoria IL 61614
United States
Tel: +1 (309) 495 2853
publishingna@ark-group.com

www.ark-group.com

Printed in the United Kingdom by Ashford Colour Press Limited, Gosport, Hampshire

ISBN: 978-1-78358-362-1

A catalogue record for this book is available from the British Library

ARK Group is a division of Wilmington plc. The company is registered in England & Wales with company number 2931372 GB. Registered office: 5th Floor, 10 Whitechapel High Street, London E1 8QS.

VAT Number: GB 899 3725 51.

Contents

Executive summary

The contemporary legal landscape is no longer a rigid hierarchy composed of limited and complacent behemoths, but rather an ecosystem, filled with a wide variety of players that facilitate disruption and revolution and jostle for clients' attention with agility and innovation. This includes – but is certainly not limited to – entities such as technology companies, consultants, alternative legal service providers, and paraprofessionals. Law firms are not the only ones in this environment that must adapt or fail; the legal department and in-house counsel, too, must transform in order to remain relevant and competitive. The world of the general counsel (GC) has already seen massive shifts – ever-increasing globalization has meant more legal issues and corporate activism, which in turn has generated new challenges and heightened demand. The GC cannot simply act in the role of outsourcer of work to external counsel, as in the past. With the growth of legal departments (it is now not uncommon for legal departments to number in the hundreds or even thousands, often formed of expensive lateral hires) the GC must now wear a number of hats, including that of the "CEO" of their department. The introduction of data analysis into the legal space and the oft-repeated mantra of "less with more" has meant that the GC must now think in terms of spend and budget more than ever before, transforming the legal department from a cost-center to a value-add. They must cultivate a breadth and scope of vision, able to organize and lead their department as an innovator. The flourishing legal ops role also provides yet another challenge for the GC. As the incorporation of legal ops within the law department becomes increasingly essential, the GC must work to ensure alignment and manage change.

The present time has been hailed as the golden age of in-house lawyering, yet – and perhaps because of this – it is an uncertain and challenging time for the GC. *Tipping Point: Transformation and Innovation in the Legal Department* is intended as a handbook for the GC looking to build a truly modern legal department and revolutionize their role. Encompassing aspects from leveraging influence with the c-suite to reimagining organizational hierarchies and seeking the right operational professional, this publication features contributions from those at the frontiers of the profession as it transforms and embraces new areas of expertise.

"Legal operations" has become a buzzword, meaning different things to different people, legal departments and law firms. The Corporate Legal Operations Consortium (CLOC) now reports that two-thirds of the Fortune 100 are among its members; however, there is a wide difference in the definition of what successful legal operations means and its level of use. In chapter one, Merry Neitlich – founding partner of EM Consulting – explores the essence of legal operations in terms of collaboration, predictability, and innovation between the legal department and the law firm. Real and lasting change cannot be accomplished without understanding and implementing successful change process management strategies, which must be a part of the collaborative process. Readers will learn the approach necessary to gain a deeper understanding of the goals and outcomes that will benefit the three-legged stool of an organization, its legal department, and its outside law firms.

The theme of collaboration continues in chapter two, as Gonzalo Ruiz – an award-winning in-house lawyer who has occupied high-profile roles at The Coca Cola Company and PlayStation – tackles the issues that can emerge when engaging with external counsel, identifying frequent key challenges and delineating a practical roadmap to building meaningful and productive relationships.

The general counsel is a key advisor to the board, with the potential for a high degree of influence. However, this can only be built over time. The GC is likely to have contact with the board only for major matters or in times of crisis; as such, they need its respect and trust. This brings its own set of challenges: how does the GC build the right degree of trust and develop the requisite credibility, and over what matters? How can they work with the key members of the board, and what can be done if the relationship goes wrong? In chapter three, Ian White – a member of Sherwood psf Consulting and former chief legal officer and company secretary – utilizes his expertise to address these pressing questions, which will have relevance for any modern GC.

Analytics in the legal world is here to stay; it is now vital to not only introduce data measuring systems, but to also effectively implement them. However, it is not always easy to know where to start. In chapter four, Aaron Katzel – president and CEO of The Better Legal Infrastructure Project LLC – outlines which metrics matter and why, providing a launchpad from which a GC can build and grow a mature analytics system tailored to their specific department's needs, as well as looking ahead to what the future holds in the form of predictive legal analytics.

In today's competitive environment, general counsels are under increasing pressure to make contracting simpler, faster, and more useful; however, challenging times are fantastic opportunities for leadership and innovation. Some actions that can bring significant value include implementing visual contracts and no-touch contracting, using contracting principles to streamline negotiations, leveraging analytics and "outsights" to support the case for change, and increasing commercial capabilities of all who touch contracting. This is the time for GCs to drive the sort of changes that transform "ease of doing business" and redefine the role of the legal function, and in chapter five Peggy Chang Barber – Americas CEO and general counsel for the International Association of Contract and Commercial Management (IACCM) – utilizes her expertise to demonstrate how to get started.

Agile methodologies got their start with technology teams; however, in recent years, all components of an organization have embraced Agile's light-touch yet high-impact approach. In chapter six, John E Grant – founder of the Agile Attorney Network – gives real-world examples of corporate legal departments using Agile to improve the speed and quality of legal services delivery. He explores the four foundational principles of Agile for legal; explains how Agile simultaneously empowers project management, process improvement, and data-driven decision-making; and introduces the kanban board: the primary tool in the Agile toolset. He concludes with concrete steps for introducing Agile to a legal team, potential pitfalls to watch out for, and technologies that can empower your Agile transition.

Many large organizations have a procurement department dedicated to sourcing legal services. The benefits of legal procurement go well beyond just cost-cutting: having dedicated professionals trained in data analysis and sourcing technology to manage spending and increase efficiency in hiring outside counsel also frees up in-house counsel to focus on what they were trained to do – the actual legal work. In chapter seven, Dr Silvia Hodges Silverstein and Dr Lena Campagna – executive director and research and education director of the Buying Legal Council – showcases procurement's critical impact on strategic management of outside spend and how legal departments can move away from the traditional "passive" approach to managing legal spend to a more "active" or even "collaborative" approach. Readers are also introduced to different legal spend management initiatives, which range from simple process or policy changes to more complex and comprehensive programs.

The emergence and evolution of the role of operations executives within corporate law departments represent a new phase of development. Like every sort of innovation, however, this brings its own challenges. How should general counsel and chief legal officers utilize that resource? How can an operations executive enable the general counsel to serve the business more effectively? In chapter eight, Steven A Lauer, principal of Lauer & Associates, and Ken Vermilion, principal of The Vermilion Group Strategic Legal Management LLC, will address these pressing and timely questions, laying out some applicable strategies which will empower the GC to fully make use of the opportunities presented by the operations executive and realize the legal department's full potential and value.

Most corporations have opted for a model based on some version of a three-legged stool, dependent on size and complexity of the corporation: business lawyers, functional experts, and regional specialists. However, as legal departments evolve and engage with more complex matters, urgent questions arise: under what circumstances should GCs emphasize one component of this model over another? Considering emerging trends that require new capabilities, should the three-legged stool format be reconsidered? In chapter nine Jeffrey Neuman – senior vice president, general counsel and corporate secretary of Tronox Limited – addresses these important issues and more, delving into new possibilities and functions on the edge of core law department functionality that GCs should consider when structuring their own legal divisions, including cyber security, environmental resources management, and executive compensation.

If you look at an organizational chart, everything is neat and arranged into lines and boxes; however, this is not realistic or particularly innovative. Instead, in chapter ten, Patrick J Lamb – co-founder of ElevateNext Law and Valorem Law Group, and vice president of Elevate Services – proposes that legal departments should think of themselves functioning as a solar system, with the GC as the sun and the department's people and firms inhabiting an elliptical orbit dependent on which issues and tasks are prioritized. He examines the practices and components that will bring a legal department closer to this innovative model and into the future, drawing from the real-world examples of Univar and Microsoft and their efforts to remain contemporary and competitive.

About the authors

Peggy Chang Barber is the Americas CEO and general counsel for the International Association of Contract and Commercial Management (IACCM), a global non-profit focused on enabling organizations and professionals achieve world-class standards in their trading relationships. A passionate advocate for the importance of contracting to business success, Peggy enjoys developing innovative solutions to complex challenges that drive contracting and commercial excellence. Before joining IACCM, Peggy was vice president and associate general counsel at Hewlett Packard, where she developed expertise in strategic contracting, commercial and competition law, corporate transactions, business operations, and organizational performance optimization. She successfully led global projects in contracting simplification and contracting intelligence and represented Hewlett Packard Enterprise as lead commercial counsel in many corporate transactions, including the separation of Hewlett-Packard Company and spin-merger with CSC that formed DXC. Peggy graduated from The University of Texas in Austin with a law degree, MBA, and Finance and Mathematics degrees. She is a member of the Texas and DC bars and holds an Interim Top-Secret security clearance.

Dr Lena Campagna is research and education director of the international trade organization Buying Legal Council and an assistant professor in the department of Sociology and Criminal Justice at Caldwell University in New Jersey. She has extensive experience in project coordination and community outreach, mixed methods research, and program evaluation. Lena has published in peer-reviewed academic journals in social science research as well as authored educational articles on the buying of legal services. Lena holds a PhD in Sociology from the University of Massachusetts Boston, a Master's degree in American Studies from the University of Massachusetts Boston, and a Bachelor's Degree in Marketing Communication from Emerson College.

Dr Silvia Hodges Silverstein is the executive director of the Buying Legal Council, the international trade organization for legal procurement, and adjunct professor at Columbia Law School and Fordham Law School. Dr Hodges Silverstein co-authored the Harvard Business School case studies *GlaxoSmithKline: Sourcing Complex Professional Services* on the company's legal procurement initiative, and *Riverview Law: Applying Business Sense to the Legal Market* on the new model law firm. She has authored many articles on law firm management and is also the author/editor of several books, including the *Legal Procurement Handbook and Buying Legal: Procurement Insights and Practice*. She is the publisher of *Winning Proposals – The Essential Guide for Law Firms and Legal Services Providers*. She earned her PhD at Nottingham Law School (UK), holds a master's degree in business from Universität Bayreuth (Germany) and Warwick Business School (UK), and an undergraduate degree (economics) from Universität Bayreuth.

Aaron Katzel is an award-winning legal innovator, counselor and chief operating officer, who has been helping companies solve their most vexing legal and operational challenges for over 20 years. Since 2017, he has served as a trusted partner to businesses and law firms seeking to navigate the changing legal marketplace as the founder and CEO of The Better Legal Infrastructure Project LLC. In this capacity, Aaron helps clients understand and pursue opportunities to obtain better results and value in their delivery and consumption of legal services, and has designed and led initiatives that saved clients more than $1 billion while maintaining or improving legal outcomes. Aaron began his career as a transactional lawyer before encountering the opportunity to join the growing legal operations field, serving first as chief of staff to AIG's general counsel and then as the company's head of legal operations. Between 2012 and 2017, Aaron developed and led one of the industry's most recognized and innovative legal operations teams. In that role, Aaron and his team pioneered award-winning strategies that deployed data-driven, highly automated, scalable, market-based tools to price legal services. They also created the industry's first real-time, national, self-service legal analytics platform, automated over 100 separate legal processes, and managed the largest legal e-billing implementation ever completed.

Patrick J Lamb is one of the founding members of Valorem Law Group and later a founder of ElevateNext Law, as well as a vice president of Elevate Services, a global law company. Pat spent 18 years at an AmLaw

100 firm, including several years as an equity partner, before leaving the firm to join a litigation boutique where he spent seven years, including six as a member of the firm's management committee. During these years, he was an avid proponent of budgeting and non-hourly fee arrangements. Ultimately coming to the conclusion that firms could not exist in both the hourly and non-hourly worlds, Pat and three colleagues – all big firm refugees – formed Valorem, which began in January 2008 as a non-hourly, value-fee firm. Seeking the ability to provide scaled solutions to client problems, Pat and his partner Nicole Auerbach formed ElevateNext Law to work in alignment with Elevate Services, providing clients a full range of service. Described by one in-house lawyer as "one of the few lawyers who gets it", Pat was named a legal rebel by the American Bar Association in 2009 and is a frequent speaker on value fees and the role of project management in the successful use of value fees. He began writing the popular blog "In Search Of Perfect Client Service" in 2005.

Steven A Lauer is an independent consultant to corporate law departments and law firms on the value of legal service and related topics. He spent over two years as corporate counsel for Global Compliance Services in Charlotte, North Carolina, specializing in data protection and privacy and general corporate matters. Previously, he was director of integrity research for Integrity Interactive Corporation, where he conducted research, wrote whitepapers, and worked with clients on issues related to corporate ethics and compliance programs. Before that, he consulted with corporate law departments and law firms on issues related to how in-house and outside counsel work together and spent over 13 years as an in-house attorney in law departments ranging in size. Besides his legal counsel work, he also spent over two years as executive vice president, deputy editor and publisher of *The Metropolitan Corporate Counsel*, a monthly journal for in-house attorneys. Steve has authored numerous articles on compliance, the relations between in-house and outside attorneys, the selection of counsel by corporate clients, the evaluation of legal service, litigation management, and other topics relevant to corporate compliance programmes and corporate legal service. Many of his articles are posted on his website at www.thevalue-ablelawyer.com. He has organised and spoken at numerous conferences in respect of those subjects.

Merry Neitlich is the founder and managing partner of EM Consulting, a leader in law firm marketing and business development solutions.

With over 25 years of experience, Merry provides clients with tools to grow relationships and successfully identify, court and convert targets into clients. She consults with law firms wishing to overcome resistance and implement successful legal operations programs. Merry has extensive experience coaching attorneys in business development in order to grow their practices. She has interviewed hundreds of in-house counsels across the country for law firm clients in order to enhance relationships and client satisfaction. Merry offers training programs in business development, legal operations, client retention and satisfaction programs. In 2017, Merry was inducted into the LMA Hall of Fame and was inducted into the College of Law Practice Management in 2012.

Jeffrey N Neuman is currently the senior vice president, general counsel and corporate secretary for Tronox Limited, a NYSE-listed mining and chemical company with significant operations in the US, South Africa, Australia and the Netherlands. At Tronox, Jeff oversees Tronox's legal and regulatory affairs. Prior to joining Tronox, Jeff spent 16 years at Honeywell International in a variety of legal positions, including as its corporate secretary and deputy general counsel and the general counsel of Honeywell's $6 billion chemical division. Prior to moving in-house, Jeff was an M&A lawyer at Davis, Polk & Wardwell. Before law school, Jeff spent six years in the investment banking division of Merrill Lynch, with significant stints in New York, Tokyo and London. Jeff has a BA from Wesleyan University, an MA in Asian Studies from Harvard University, and a JD from Northwestern University.

Gonzalo Ruiz is an award-winning in-house legal counsel with over two decades of global legal and business experience, carrying high-profile roles at The Coca-Cola Company and Sony Interactive Entertainment. Gonzalo has gained comprehensive business acumen and an outstanding cultural awareness partnering closely with senior business executives and cross-functional leadership teams across multiple jurisdictions.

Ken Vermilion currently is the principal at The Vermilion Group Strategic Legal Management LLC. He specializes in providing middle-market legal departments with strategic planning and operational guidance. He has also co-authored *The Value-Able Law Firm*, published by and available through the ABA Business Law Section. Prior to launching The Vermilion Group, Ken was a founding director in the Houston office of Duff & Phelps Legal Management Consulting practice. He has more than 16 years' experience of in-house legal department senior management operations with two Fortune100 retail companies, where he focused on improving business performance and reducing costs through a variety of techniques including the implementation of progressive strategies, leveraging the use of technology, and the development of effective and uncomplicated management reports and metrics. Ken's expertise is highly sought after by legal industry service providers, and has contributed to the development of emerging new products for corporate legal departments, such as a legal spend management solution with international capabilities. He has been a speaker on the topics of corporate change management, data analytics and metrics. Ken earned his BS degree from Northern Illinois University.

Ian White has been the chief legal officer and/or company secretary for both listed and major private companies. This has led to developing an expertise in corporate governance and working with boards on effectiveness and performance. He has been involved in a number of board evaluations, both internally and externally. Ian now works as a consultant both on an interim and specific assignment basis. Over the last two years he has undertaken a number of board evaluations for FTSE 100/250 companies, as well as for private organizations. In addition, in 2016 he spent six months as an internal governance consultant for a FTSE 100 International Bank working on board effectiveness and governance matters generally for the Holdings Board. In the corporate world, Ian spent the majority of his time in the financial services sector (principally asset management) with roles such as group legal counsel/ company secretary of Perpetual, interim chief legal officer for Openwork Limited (formerly Allied Dunbar), and interim chief legal officer in the UK for Allianz Global Investors. Ian has also worked in other sectors and was group general counsel/company secretary of the Wilkinson Group. He is also a member of Sherwood psf Consulting.

Chapter 1:
Creating a collaborative win using legal operations

By Merry Neitlich, founder and managing partner of EM Consulting

Managing real collaboration and change

The practice of law is changing – of that there is no doubt. Legal departments – both attorneys and legal operation professionals – are doing more than simply asking outside law firms to develop a deeper understanding of their needs. After identifying the wishes of the internal stakeholders, legal departments are increasingly seeking solutions that also meet the needs of the company.

Law firm partners that embrace true collaboration find opportunities not only to enhance client relationships, but also seek ways to solve corporate business problems. Law firms can approach clients now and be innovators. Someone is probably talking to those clients about how to deliver legal services that are a win-win for the firm and legal department. A law firm doesn't want to find out down the road they lost clients because they were late to this party. The primary goal of these meaningful conversations must focus on how to make legal engagements work better for the client. This is the nugget driving innovation and change. Clients not only want more meaningful collaboration, but also increased predictability, efficiency and innovation. *These are the underpinnings of legal operations.* All stakeholders must become trained and skilled at exploring issues that yield better business solutions.

For over 25 years, internationally renowned legal futurist Richard Susskind has been researching and opining on alternative ways law firms might work best with their clients. In his book *Tomorrow's Lawyers,* Susskind writes: "Law firms in the coming decades will be driven relentlessly by their clients to find a better way to deliver legal services." All his books, lectures and keynote addresses have intimated for decades that law firms must change from the traditional billable hour and become more focused on service delivery based on client preferences, creating better efficiencies, using more technologies, and offering predictability.

During the last several decades, many feel law firms were and are calling the shots. They primarily bill by the hour, grudgingly discuss alternative ways of delivering their services, and raise their hourly rates almost annually. From the legal department's vantage point, an hourly fee-based model does not encourage true partnering; rather, it tends to focus on profitability for law firms. Creating true alternative fee arrangements generally turns out to be disappointing for in-house counsel, as typically nothing more gets offered than perhaps a 15 percent discount on the hourly billing rate. In-house counsel have been frustrated at not being able to change processes and service delivery options. They want the predictability and efficiency that is not championed by the billable hour.

And so, the term "legal operations" took on a deeper meaning.

Out of their frustration, about seven years ago a group of in-house counsel from larger corporations started to meet informally. They expressed their specific frustrations with how their departments were run and delved into issues surrounding the way legal services were being delivered from law firms. Up to this point, legal departments owned a fair share of blame for the dysfunction and inefficiencies in the system, as they didn't know what to do to change things; they just wanted to create an easier and more productive way to work. These soon-to-be change agents started to share information, processes, and technologies such as e-billing, e-discovery, and knowledge management to create better efficiencies. In addition, they discussed how they might work with outside law firms more proactively and in a way to minimize costs, frustrations and repetitive tasks. They wished law firms would approach them to ask what would make the delivery of services better for the client. These visionary leaders became the founders of the Corporate Legal Operations Consortium (CLOC), and included Connie Brenton from NetApp, Mary O'Carroll from Google, Jeff Franke from Yahoo, Christine Coats from Oracle, Lisa Konie from Adobe, Steve Harmon from Cisco, and Brian Hupp from Facebook. In 2016, CLOC incorporated as a nonprofit trade association; it has become one of the fastest growing nonprofit legal organizations in the world. Since incorporating, CLOC has grown to include over 2000 members, 1000 member companies, two-thirds of the Fortune 100; it spans 40 states, 42 countries, and 26 regional groups.

"Everybody keeps saying the legal services industry is broken, that radical change is badly needed, but only a few – like industry thought leader Richard Susskind – were even looking at the issues industry-wide. No one had tried to set forth what true north is for this industry. Most legal departments focused on law firms as the only ones really needing to change," said Jeff Franke, former assistant general counsel of global legal operations at Yahoo, founding member of CLOC as well as its former general counsel and corporate secretary. But the challenges the corporate legal services industry face go way beyond the billable hour, and beyond the intransigence of law firms to change their basic operating model. Franke explained, "We need lots of change with respect to the six core ecosystem players," which includes:

- Corporations;
- Law firms;
- Regulators;
- Law schools;
- Tech providers; and
- Outside service providers.

Many corporations have started making changes, and we will see more radical transformation over the next three to five years than we have in the last 20. A relatively small number of proactive law firms have taken the time to understand what legal operations means and how it can enhance client (and even potential client) relationships. By entering into discussions of a symbiotic nature, these legal departments and law firms are creating win-win outcomes.

The industry has come a come a long way from the days when GCs were seen primarily as risk managers who relied almost exclusively on outside counsel to support a corporation's legal needs. Today, 40 – 60 percent of all corporate legal work is done in-house. As GCs have brought legal support in-house to meet the mandate to deliver strategic and efficient legal support, operations excellence has become a critical necessity. Unfortunately, historically the only way to develop that excellence was from the ground up: legal operations did not exist as a discipline. No one offered a "how-to guide" on this complex topic.

With the mandate to "run legal like a business," thoughtful in-house operations professionals got to work defining the space. It was initially a slow evolution of legal ops. CLOC – through its members and leadership – quickly created a thoughtful, effective base of knowledge, templates, benchmarking capability, and best practice. Their efforts led to the creation of CLOC's 12 Core Competencies for legal operations excellence. Information from seminars, conferences, webinars, templates, articles, local meetings and materials are helping legal departments and other core ecosystem players better understand what corporate legal departments need and want.

The Association of Corporate Counsel (ACC) has jumped into legal operations in a big way as well. Amar Sarwal, chief legal officer and senior VP of advocacy and legal services, spearheads the ACC Legal Operations program and has aligned it fully with the ACC Value Challenge. In addition to supporting and advancing the legal operations profession, ACC views its role as assisting the general counsel's office to fully leverage legal operations. According to Amar, "Our role will not only make the legal operations function more coherent, but also help unify the process for its stakeholders. We help many legal departments that have previously not had a legal ops function open up to the possibilities. Wherever a department finds itself in this process, we can share concepts, leadership strategies, conferences, tools, and written guidelines to enhance the legal ops function. Both the ACC program and CLOC are committed to the success of the legal department."

ACC legal ops focuses in two areas. It offers assistance to onboard new legal ops professionals sharing and leveraging materials and knowledge with a foundational toolkit, its Maturity Model. ACC also helps advance those legal operations counsels already immersed by providing continued assistance, strategies and information to get them to the next level.

What legal departments can do

Jeff Franke added, "Many in-house legal operation counsels feel a legal department might begin by defining the largest areas of frustration working with outside law firms, vendors and legal project management. Ask your law firms to step up. Invite them to visit and share ideas how you might work together to create better communication and stronger relationships. Legal ops in-house professionals anticipate more and more law firms will get the message and proactively approach them to find ways to create mutually beneficial strategies.

"As an example, we spend money just to pull stats for our quarterly reviews. It would be wonderful if law firms proactively did this for us. Come to a quarterly review with statistics. Law firms need to understand that as legal departments are tasked with running a business within our company's business, we need law firms on board too."

Those working in-house looking to deepen their involvement might explore CLOC's 12 Core Competencies, selecting just a few to start the analysis process. What technologies do you already have and which ones are most important? Which will relieve your biggest frustrations and headaches with outside firms? Do you have a legal operations team in-house devoted to creating better efficiencies and partnering with outside firms? How might you start this process?

Pratik Patel – VP of innovation and products at Elevate Services – says that without a legal operations function, the result is often over-worked teams and inefficient practice of law. "Legal operations can tame the chaos of running the legal department," says Patel, who provides consulting services and technology implementation to in-house legal departments. "Without the legal ops function, lawyers are forced to design and develop the business aspects of their function in self-service models or in silos, often leading to limited or non-existent processes and fairly pedestrian use of technology."

Pratik explains that developing a framework around legal operations and prioritizing the competency areas can build efficiencies that better align with a company's business objectives. He recommends four simple steps to get started:

1. Identify the law department's business objectives;
2. Gauge each core competency's ability to influence those objectives;
3. Assess the overall levels of maturity in each area; and
4. Focus on the maturity areas most likely to "move the needle" towards your objectives.

Today, the legal operations function at major corporations has migrated from an uncoordinated disparate set of actions by individual players to a more carefully defined, cross-disciplinary profession loosely aligned across hundreds of companies and government entities. The focus is on changing not only the way corporate legal departments deliver legal services, but on the way in which the whole corporate legal services industry should function. Corporate legal departments are in the driver's seat.

There is no doubt that legal operations is a growing force in the competitive landscape for law firms to keep and expand client relationships. Many predict that 2019 will be a watershed year, in which we see many more legal departments and law firms jump into legal operations; for those already involved, the prediction is the level of use will significantly deepen. Legal operations is a partnership between legal departments and their outside law firms. If the steady and impressive growth of CLOC membership and legal operations professionals who take advantage of the numerous legal ops offerings from ACC continues, it will not be too many years in the future when law firms who resisted learning about legal operations will wish they hadn't.

The successful delivery of legal operations can happen with law firms of all sizes

Legal departments, at times, want to work with law firms, of various sizes in a more collaborative fashion. But sometimes, mid- and small-size law firms wonder if companies are interested in hearing from them. The answer is yes. Numerous large law firms, even the Am Law 100 and 200 firms, are not yet using legal ops as an umbrella to grow their practices. The door is open for firms of all sizes as in-house counsels may be open to a law firm initiating the conversation about creating innovation and efficiencies. This quote from the senior director of legal operations at a Fortune 500 Company sums up her perspective on how a law firm can assist a legal department to create more successful relationships with mid-size and smaller law firms:

"It's great that some smaller and mid-size law firms are incorporating legal operations principles. At our company, we are open to considering smaller firms. Sometimes, working with larger firms can be a turn off because of their complicated infrastructure and poor service. Mid-size and smaller firms can be more facile and easier to work with, especially if they take the time to understand our company, see where we are headed, and how they can work with us to create better efficiencies. In fact, some corporations want to try out relationships with smaller firms but finding the right firm can be a challenge."

Consider collaborative-type questions in-house counsels might ask law firms as they explore legal operations together:

1. How has your firm worked with clients (and targeted non-clients) to create better efficiencies and more predictability in fees?
2. What technologies does your firm have that assist in this process?
3. Is your firm using any AI as it delivers more efficient work to clients?
4. How can your firm can add more value?
5. Do you have suggestions that will keep your initial budget on track?
6. How can your firm help create legal solutions that meet our corporate goals and business strategies?

In some cases, neither the law firm nor the legal department are proficient in these ideas, but an exploratory conversation can be very proactive. The conversation should be all about the pain points of the in-house counsel. Together, they can explore alternative solutions and cost-effective strategies.

Just discussing change has never been an effective strategy for making change. For decades law firms have looked in the rearview mirror and clung to the history of how things were done. These days law firms are understanding the directive from legal departments that change is needed. Conversations about legal operations can help make the positive changes legal departments are seeking.

A solution for creating more predictability in big ticket litigation

The boutique law firm of Klein & Wilson, a small trial powerhouse based in Newport Beach, CA, created an innovative solution working on significant trial matters. The firm developed a process to help clients wrap their arms around a clear path and associated costs of large cases through its Litigation Analysis Memo (LAM).

Partnering with clients to write the LAM, Klein & Wilson prepares a detailed factual background referencing key documents necessary to understand the events leading to litigation. After the client approves the factual background, Klein & Wilson prepares a comprehensive legal analysis and litigation strategy (goals identified; paths to reach goals presented; legal issues identified and resolved; anticipated discovery explained; anticipated motions identified; damages analyzed if possible; potential experts listed; strengths and weaknesses reviewed; case theme developed; and thorough budget presented based on assumptions). The client reviews the LAM and decides whether to contest or settle the case.

By thinking through a case upfront, Klein & Wilson efficiently lays out a plan that accomplishes clients' goals and creates a meaningful budget – not just numbers on a paper nobody takes seriously. If the client-approved assumptions are correct, and the client has accurately presented the facts, Klein & Wilson's litigation budgets are usually within 20 percent of the client's actual expenses. Early and comprehensive case analysis leads to predictable outcomes and minimizes discovery and motion expenses.

Preparing a LAM at the outset of a case is one of the reasons Klein & Wilson has over a 90 percent win rate at trial. The Klein & Wilson LAM has impressed clients and adversaries alike. After Klein & Wilson settled a large case for a small client where the future of the company was at stake, the Fortune 500 defendant (which paid the settlement) asked Klein & Wilson to represent it in future matters. There was one condition: the Fortune 500 Company wanted to see the LAM Klein & Wilson prepared which had been so devastating. The LAM notebook had been on the table at every deposition and hearing. The firm's small client was so thrilled with its settlement that it not only gave permission to, but actively encouraged, Klein & Wilson to show the LAM to the former adversary. At one point in a deposition, a frustrated witness answered in response to a question: "If it is in your damn notebook, it happened, OK?"

It should not be surprising that an innovative firm like Klein & Wilson uses a LAM to plan case strategy and develop a meaningful budget. The real question is why other firms do not prepare similar support documents. Firm partner Mark Wilson commented, "We plan case strategy with our trial opening statement in mind. By keeping our eye on the critical points we need to win the trial, we save our clients a substantial amount of money. Cases are won and lost on pivotal issues, not minutiae which distract many attorneys."

Some law firms are equipping their partners with legal ops professionals who can either support on specific matters or generally assist with advancing the legal operations conversation. This is a change that an increasingly large number of firms are considering.

MassMutual implements successful legal operations: a case study

Christine Juhasz, legal operations leader for MassMutual (a mutual life insurance company), meets quarterly with many law firms that the company does business with to help improve legal operations collaboratively. These meetings are sacred to the legal ops professionals and the law firm partners. Additionally, MassMutual and key law firms collaborate in strategic process improvement sessions. This typically involves an all-day process to assess the end-to-end flow of work and information resulting in improvements for both the firm and MassMutual and a demonstration of how legal services and legal operations can mesh to create innovation and lasting, sustainable change.

MassMutual assesses many factors in selecting outside counsel. Of paramount importance is the integrity, values, skill, quality and diversity of the team handling the work. Past experience and strong endorsements from colleagues are always helpful, as well as access to data and analytics. Firms that demonstrate the ability to think outside the box and willingness to create more predictability and efficiencies based on the needs of the company and the legal division are key.

"We successfully started our journey into legal operations by listening and learning from our internal clients, understanding the end-to-end stream of work, and identifying opportunities to close strategic gaps. The need to build, store, retrieve and use our knowledge base was a real opportunity for us. We looked deeply into the capabilities of the legal division to understand how we could improve the efficiency with which we deliver advice and counsel to the company. This information helped us transform from process improvement to deeper legal operations," Christine stated.

Christine continued, "From my observations, one of the biggest areas that law firms can focus on to become more effective and efficient is to not overlook legal ops professionals in their work with attorneys. Our legal ops team is a hub of information and expertise in collaboration with legal professionals and business teams."

Making it a win for your internal clients: a case study

The legal department of a Fortune 500 company was reviewing their legal operations practices and interactions with their internal clients. Under the leadership of their senior vice president and general counsel, the department of 35 attorneys decided to ask their internal clients at the company how their services were being viewed and what could be done to improve upon them.

During the first quarter that year, 30 company executives and high-level managers were interviewed regarding their opinions on the services delivered to them by the legal department. The majority of interviews were held in-person at corporate headquarters. Several of the interviews were conducted by telephone. The participants filled out a 14-question short answer continuum-based questionnaire. This information was transferred into graphs which allowed the attorneys to visually see their service strengths and weaknesses at a glance. The in-person feedback reports combined with the statistical data provided a deeper level of knowledge.

The overall feedback was quite positive. The interview process yielded specific areas in which the services were perceived as very strong. The results also highlighted areas that needed improvement or increased communication.

Overview: comments

Over 90 percent of the respondents offered complimentary comments such as, "The legal department…

- provides strong business advice with pragmatism."
- is very proactive."
- is hard working."
- is very responsive."
- adds great value."
- provides exceptional levels of service."
- is comprised of well-respected attorneys."

Almost to the individual, respondents reported that the attorneys in the department were caring, friendly, and concerned. The attorneys were also perceived as providing valuable information while being dedicated to their clients' individual projects. Legal services were viewed as having significantly improved over the last five years.

Areas for improvement

Most of those interviewed felt that the attorneys were as thinly stretched as possible. This caused some to request that the legal department explore options to improve response time to better handle their questions and matters. There were numerous comments from individuals requesting more time with the attorneys to conduct planning and brainstorming sessions. There were a variety of responses that addressed the need to improve the department's public relations and communications. A common theme from most respondents was the desire to create more predictability in fees from their outside law firms. Some commented there was redundancy and inefficiencies in the legal work delivered. They wondered how their outside law firms could get more focused on the business needs of the company. More than a few wished the attorneys would work with their outside firms to help them get a better perspective of the company's goals.

Although most respondents felt the attorneys worked to structure win-win solutions to legal problems, more than a few wished the attorneys would continue to expand their knowledge of their particular operating group's needs. Some interviewees wished their legal department lawyers would increase their knowledge of where the company was headed they could be more proactive in helping to achieve identified business goals.

Based on the feedback, the legal department developed the following areas in which to improve upon the delivery of their services:

Better internal communications

The legal department considered implementing mechanisms to increase communication with all of its clients. Strategies included:

- Creating an internal listserv to keep all apprised of new initiatives and the state of current projects;
- Meeting with each operating group to develop strategies to create a more global, big picture understanding of their needs;
- Obtaining more feedback from each operating group to plan future services and budgets;
- Creating an electronic mechanism to delineate the areas of expertise of each of the attorneys. This communication piece will also offer suggestions for streamlining services; and
- Making a presentation to each operating group to share the findings on how this client feedback process may impact each specific operating group.

Better workflow options

Many comments were received indicating that the attorneys were "very stretched" with regard to their time restraints. Being conscious of budgetary issues, the department reviewed the attorneys' time allocations and usage and explored options to provide more time for individual clients.

Relationships with outside law firms

The legal department examined how it interfaced with its outside law firms. They developed an educational program inviting select law firms in to discuss the broader business goals of the company and also to find processes to streamline work flow and the delivery of product from the firms.

Conclusions and next steps

The results of the client feedback interviews were very positive. The overwhelming majority of the feedback was highly complimentary and demonstrated that the legal department was serving its clients well. The feedback also allowed the legal department to examine areas that needed to be improved upon and several areas that needed strong follow-up.

One month after the interviews were delivered, the legal department (staff, paralegals, and attorneys) participated in a half-day retreat. We evaluated the results of the Client Feedback Assessment Program and planned appropriate follow-up steps.

The legal department received positive feedback from the corporation's executives due to the strong and specific follow up that occurred. It became apparent that the department was perceived as a true value-added service to this corporation.

Why are there frequently problems with the implementation of legal ops, and what can be done to tackle them?

The reasons generally have little to do with the merit of the program. Rather, the resistance to change, or keeping the status quo, has to do with concern over actually *using* the new innovation. Questions as to how individuals will be evaluated on their effective use of the innovation, and when significant competency of the change is expected, are often the real culprits of resistance. Oftentimes the legal department or law firm will provide training, practice and a breakin period for the innovation to be learned. Why, then, don't these factors eliminate the struggle in accomplishing the innovation?

Concepts such as corporate culture, history, inertia and levels of concern over the new change and varying levels of effective use may all come to play as to why the innovation is producing more negative feelings than positive outcomes.

In many instances, a legal department or a law firm may try to rush through this process without the assistance of training and research. An innovation might seem urgent and justified to a committee and it is pushed into being. This can dramatically raise the level of concern of participants. When a department steps back and explores individual concerns, the probability of a shortened and successful implementation greatly increases.

How the CBAM Model creates successful change

In the musical *The Music Man*, actor Robert Preston plays the part of the swindling salesman selling band instruments in a small town around the turn of the century. Preston tells the parents that, in order for their children to master a piece of music, they need only use the Think Method – aka, simply thinking about that particular composition. If only change was so easy!

A better strategy might be to use a successful research-based change model such as the CBAM Model, which is an acronym for the Concerns Based Adoption Model, a change process model copyrighted by the Research & Development Center at The University of Texas at

Austin. Change is hard and requires long-term commitment; leaning on research-proven methods to successfully launch change can be the difference between "We talked about it" and "We did it!"

In order to create a positive transition, department-wide implementation plans should begin early in the process. Clearly stated expectations and a safe learning environment will greatly enhance the probability of success. Deal with cultural issues such as:

- What are the frontend concerns of each individual that the innovation affects?
- How might this affect each individual?
- What is expected from each person and over what time frame?
- Does this process negate or put into question some basic givens about the department's culture?

Perhaps the legal department and its internal clients might schedule meetings to deal with individual concerns. Discuss the training format from orientation to mechanical use to routine use to full integration. Allow participants to verbalize anticipated stumbling blocks and concerns. The training and implementation process might need to be reexamined and refocused several times during this process. This will effectively decrease the level of concern and increase the effective level of use of all participants.

The change process in any organization, according to the CBAM research, is fairly constant. By giving more meaningful planning time to this process, we can expect to greatly:

- Reduce training and implementation time;
- Reduce the level of concern of all participants regarding the innovation;
- Increase effective levels of use; and
- Create comradery and a sense of pride and accomplishment through the successful implementation of the innovation.

How the CBAM Model works

As more and more legal departments and law firms delve into changes designed to increase relationships with clients and potential clients, many are discovering they share concerns in implementing real and lasting change. Once internal feedback is received and assessed, a close look at how any needed changes will occur is essential.

The needed changes can grind even the most innovative idea to a pulp if proactive planning is not adequate. Those who are involved in the delivery of changes continue to discover that repairing the damage of a poorly planned innovation is costlier and more time-consuming than a carefully planned proactive approach.

The CBAM research attempts to understand (1) how people change in both their feelings about their use of new programs, and (2) what processes and characteristics of individuals and settings facilitate or inhibit the change process. The Model points out that "change is a process" by describing the process' four phases. Within every phase, there are characteristics of an effective innovation change program.

CBAM assumes that individuals grow in both their feelings toward and their use of new programs and that, in order to enhance that growth, one must tailor assistance to specific developmental needs. Individuals involved in this process usually move through three global stages in their concerns about the new approach:

1. Self-concerns manifest during introductory phases (How will this affect me?);
2. Initial use is characterized by concerns about management of the program (Will I ever get it all organized?); and
3. Only when these prior concerns are resolved do concerns about impact on learners take over (Are they learning what they need?).

Research on the CBAM has identified six stages of concern about any innovation that reflect this general trend.

Stages of concern

Stage 0	Awareness
Stage 1	Informational
Stage 2	Personal
Stage 3	Management
Stage 4	Consequence
Stage 5	Collaboration
Stage 6	Refocusing

As individuals become more familiar and comfortable with an innovation, they became more skilled and coordinated in its use, and more sensitive to its actual impact on the firm.

The **levels of use** of the innovation are the second aspect of the change process which describes individuals' actual use of the innovation.

Levels of use

LEVEL 0	Non-use
LEVEL 1	Orientation
LEVEL 2	Preparation
LEVEL 3	Mechanical use
LEVEL 4a	Routine
LEVEL 4b	Refinement
LEVEL 5	Integration
LEVEL 6	Renewal

Using the concepts from the level of concern and the level of use, we can view the change process in four phases:

1. Orientation and preparation;
2. Implementation;
3. Maintenance; and
4. Refinement.

Legal department and law firm innovations will be successful if development, training and support activities are designed according to the developmental needs of the participants. Initial activities should be directed at informational and personal concerns. Handson skill development training should occur next, followed by specific and timely problem-solving.

Finally, selfanalytical and learneroriented application activities should be recognized and held in high regard. The continuous support of participants, monitoring of progress and needs, and firmwide administrative support all greatly increase the likelihood of a truly successful innovation. Leaving out any one of these steps greatly reduces the chance for a successful implementation of the innovation.

The conclusion about legal ops

Legal departments have made it clear that the practice of law must, and in fact, is changing. Law firms and legal departments are teaming and collaborating to create and deliver better services that match the business needs of the legal department and company. Legal operations is an umbrella term used to set the stage for increased predictability, better technologies, more efficient legal services and innovation. And all of this is to create win-win legal solutions.

Chapter 2:
Building the foundation – collaboration between internal and external counsel

By Gonzalo Ruiz, international general counsel and ethics and compliance officer

I have always viewed outside counsel to be an extension of my in-house legal team; ultimately, our common goal should be achieving the business objectives through acting as enablers. I am starting from the premise that you already have an ongoing relationship with outside counsel; in this chapter, I will try to identify certain areas through which in-house counsel can further its relationships with external counsel. I will also mention some pointers to increase and enable such engagement. This outline is written from the point-of-view of an in-house counsel, with an international career spanning over 20 years.

Selecting the right partner

There are many reasons you may find yourself having to engage outside counsel, whether you need to involve someone in a very specialized area of the law; require temporary support on a particular situation, litigation, investigation or deal; or whether you are expanding into a new geography. As mentioned above, I will begin with the assumption that you already have a relationship with an external counsel, and that you have clearly mapped out your goals and priorities in that regard (including budget issues). I will therefore not go into the many strategies regarding the selection and hiring of outside counsel. That being said, I believe that it is worthwhile mentioning some very high-level thoughts on selecting new outside counsel, or maybe even re-engaging your current one(s) – in some cases, you may have a law firm that has been "grandfathered" in your organization, and may be interested in looking for alternatives.

As mentioned before, there are many selection strategies; however, in very general terms, in order to make an informed decision when looking for outside counsel I like taking the approach of interviewing them in a similar manner to an individual's job interview. In that sense, I see myself interviewing the "law firm" itself (as an institution) as well as the lawyers as individual practitioners. In that sense, I am very interested in two levels:

1) Objectively – their qualifications, experience, expertise and skills; and
2) Subjectively – the chemistry, empathy and overall feel of how well we will work together.

You may prefer a presentation, a white paper or some other type of approach, but ultimately I like to see which law firm was better prepared for the interview – demonstrating a true interest in the company and myself – and which law firm was a good listener. Ultimately, it will all boil down to the type of relationship you are looking for.

One additional thought is that (although I am not going into details of addressing budgetary issues) it should be understood that it is extremely important to set expectations and deliverables early in the engagement of outside counsel. There should be common targets and an arrangement in which both parties feel they will benefit from the relationship. The rate structure should be reasonable for the work that is being performed by outside counsel, and should take into account the right resources that are being employed (depending on the matter).

Develop institutional knowledge

For lawyers to be able to provide the most effective legal and business advice, we inevitably must know and interpret the law. However, it is just as important for us to understand our client, its products and services, the industry, the competitive landscape, and so on.

Going into a new role as in-house counsel, we must quickly learn the business and the stakeholders. As such, we have the important task of providing our outside counsel with as much information and insights as possible about our enterprise from all angles. Our "clients" (in the broad sense of the word) require that all lawyers supporting their business objectives and achieving their goals are truly strategic business partners. It is the role of the in-house counsel to transmit this spirit to outside counsel and have them ask questions that are above-and-beyond only the legal advice. From my perspective, there is a tremendous added value when lawyers go outside the comfort zone of the legal landscape and ask business questions.

The old adage "it is not what you know, but who you know" certainly comes to mind as well. Developing institutional knowledge requires time and effort. The in-house practitioners should take into account the learning curve that all new associates have within their organizations and apply that principle to their outside counsel. That means that we should consider supporting the development of knowledge about the company as well as our internal resources and stakeholders (the people).

Most companies already have vast information about them, the industry, the competitive landscape, etc. – so why not share it freely with outside counsel? In that sense, just as outside counsel shares with us some developments in law, I have always found it relevant for us (as in-house counsel) to share with them company news, industry trends, news articles, etc. For example, if your company has a newsletter, or other materials, make sure that you send it to them as well. We should not take for granted that outside counsel will be as up-to-date and with the most current news as us when it comes to our company because they have many clients. It is our responsibility to proactively engage them in that sense.

The more information you are able to share with outside counsel, the better. For instance, do they have a copy of your organizational chart? Do they understand the structure of your legal department? Try to explain some of the dynamics and stakeholders that are involved in the decision-making in your company. To me, explaining to external counsel the company's goals is as equally important as telling them about the "culture" in your organization, the "chain of command", and the "chart of authority" (formal and informal).

Consider having an "on-boarding" presentation for outside counsel just as you have for your own associates. In the past, I have involved my business colleagues in those types of presentations (including those in human resources and training departments). If you have the resources, consider having an "all-hands meeting". I would suggest taking advantage of some of the most frequently attended seminars and legal events globally (e.g. INTA, IBA) – perhaps even engage the local firm where these events are taking place, as they may be open to host the event (even if that means they will be hosting other law firms, because ultimately it also presents as an additional network opportunity for all).

Aim to develop a true sense of team

As I indicate at the very start of this chapter, external counsel is an extension of my legal team. That has always been my philosophy and I make sure that they know it. I always aspire to be an integrated and cohesive team with an open channel of communication. With time, you will build trust, which is an invaluable component of productivity and effectiveness.

When engaging external counsel, it is extremely important to determine who are the responsible lawyers (partner/s, associate/s), as well as paralegals, with the understanding that they will work throughout the lifetime of the matter. In that way, you can continue with the relationship on an ongoing basis, precisely to develop the institutional knowledge and the sense of team.

Building that true sense of team also requires the right work allocation and role assignment between internal and external resources (and this will also depend on the size and scale of your own company and legal function). The proper assignment of roles is fundamental to avoid duplicity and, even at times, having contradictory opinions when negotiating a point or giving advice to a client. We cannot afford to appear disengaged and unaligned facing third parties. To give you an example, in some of the dealings in which I have been involved, I have witnessed the other parties' internal and external counsel disagreeing at the negotiation table. In addition, some deals and projects may require outside counsel to be more visible and take the lead independently, and you must feel comfortable in delegating (some in-house counsel are not comfortable delegating even within their own organizations and teams). In other situations you may have to involve another member of the company to act as the main project lead (e.g. someone in finance and strategic planning); in those cases the alignment I am referring to is crucial. Discuss what the best approach is and come to an accord for full alignment with your external counsel, whether you will actively participate in the handling of some matters or whether you are comfortable in letting them handle some things completely on their own.

Of course, the type of work external counsel will be doing for you will help you set your expectations on the levels of engagement accordingly. I always keep in mind that the law firms have their own culture and interests in mind. Developing this true sense of team requires time and effort on our part as in-house counsel to understand external counsel's own objectives. It is truly a two-way street, and showing your outside counsel that you also care for their business is important.

Celebrate victories (and identify areas of opportunity)

Once a project is completed, a good way of developing this sense of team is to take the time to recognize and celebrate "victories" and address areas of opportunity immediately in furtherance of future engagements. I think it is important to give and receive feedback at both ends of the spectrum. If you are truly trying to develop a long-term relationship, it is key to do this systematically. We all like to get a sense of accomplishment, and in my experience conveying clearly to outside counsel how much you appreciate their support goes a long way.

I have always been passionate about the products and brands I have represented, and my hope would be that my external counsel would share into that passion. My personal philosophy about work overall is that the results are very important; however, so is the experience and the journey as a whole.

Rules of engagement: policies, guidelines and day-to-day communications

"The devil is in the details" is another expression that comes to mind. Having a clear path of how you will interact with outside counsel – and even with certain individual members on their end –is extremely important for purposes of being effective and the most productive.

In pursuit of a more effective and productive collaboration and alignment, I like to keep my communications with external counsel as streamlined as possible. To that effect, I like establishing "guidelines", "rules of engagement", processes, forms, etc., that can be conducive for the interactions. For instance, I personally do not like outside counsel preparing long memos (unless asked to do so).

I highly recommend drafting "guidelines" for purposes of standardization of day-to-day interactions and communications (more about this below). These "guidelines for outside counsel" will help provide a general framework of the interaction and relationship. Suffice to say, the guidelines should include compliance with all of your company's policies (e.g. code of business conduct, supplier guiding principles, fees and billing policies for vendors, etc.).

The guidelines should include:

- How to address conflicts of interest, including any conflict waivers.
- Principal point of contact, both at the company as well as the law firm. In my experience, all legal work should originate with and through the legal function. Even if outside counsel is approached by someone from the company directly outside of the legal function for a project, outside counsel should immediately notify you before they proceed with any work. In addition, it is always a good idea to have one person that can point you in the right direction within their organization. Of course, you should always be able to reach

out to anybody on the firm's side, but it is very effective to have one point of contact. This is particularly relevant for the purposes of proper delegation. Ultimately, you want to engage the right level of experience and seniority without compromising quality.

- Power-of-attorney ("POA"). In some jurisdictions and depending on the subject matter (i.e. litigation), your outside counsel will require a power-of-attorney, so make sure that you fully understand what is required under local law (e.g. legalization, notarization, apostille, just the signature, etc.). Although some law firms like to have POAs with the right to delegate further within their law firm (fully understand that it gives them flexibility), I personally do not like to provide such *carte blanche* and rather keep a limited scope (otherwise you lose track of who is actually representing your company). It is up to you whether you prioritize flexibility or control. In addition, outside of the scope of that POA, also establish a chart of authority/settlement authority.
- Media inquiries protocol. My rule of thumb is that external counsel should always decline to comment on any matters they are handling (or handled) and refer them to my company. Suffice to say, some outside counsel really enjoy time in the spotlight. However, you definitively want to check with your internal public relations team as to what should be the policy when addressing media inquiries and even using your case(s) as examples in seminars and in the classroom. You do not want unnecessary showing-off in some of your matters (not even if you are successful in them).
- Non-advertisement, no endorsement. Some law firms like to proactively advertise that they have certain clients. This is directly connected with the previous point – engage your public affairs and communications (or public relations) team to determine what is best for your company.

Keep these principles in mind when you request from outside counsel their own communications (as detailed below).

Day-to-day communications

When asking a question from external counsel, it is important that you explain your issue(s) with as much detail as possible and with the necessary business context and background. Outside counsel are not privy to the dozens of internal meetings and e-mail exchanges, and the overall background in some of the deals. To that effect, you should spend the time to convey your situation coherently, clearly and effectively. As a general framework, I use the following:

- Explain urgency and importance (including deadlines);
- Frame the issue precisely;
- Summarize the issues and facts; and
- Stakeholders (internal and external).

This framework will help outside counsel organize their response in a much clear fashion.

Email

In this day and age, we tend to over-communicate (e-mail, instant messages, social media, etc.). Having a clear understanding of what should be the channels of communications with outside counsel, and how you share information, is very important.

Inevitably, we still rely heavily on e-mails. If we have to practice what we preach, we should not be abusing the use of e-mail. What is the most productive and cost-effective manner of communicating? Be selective, and effective, on when to use e-mail and when it may be better to pick up the phone. If we foresee that a conversation may take more than three e-mails, maybe then we should consider picking-up the phone, because there are certainly times in which I have found myself having a ten-minute conversation that resolves a huge thread of e-mails.

Of course, again, email is the most common manner of communicating with outside counsel. To that effect, I highly recommend establishing an effective email practice for purposes of productivity and effectiveness. If you have frequent interaction with outside counsel, consider the standardization of certain communications (e.g. instructions to file for a trademark registration, trademark searches, etc.).

I always aim to have "easy-to-read" email communications with internal clients and with my outside counsel (think of it as the "less is more" approach). For example, external counsel should communicate to me in the simplest manner possible and sometimes even using plain English, because I will eventually have to transmit that opinion to my internal clients. In that sense, I like the simplicity of having the conclusion at the beginning of an opinion and, if applicable, the inclusion of proposed solutions.

Just as important is the format in which an e-mail is sent: consider how the recipient(s) will read the message, whether they are traveling and, if so, they will be reading it on a mobile device. Is English their first language? How many recipients must be included in the message? There is more about this below, but suffice to say there are various elements that can contribute to better e-mail etiquette, including a proper subject line, how to structure the body of the email itself, and other things we can do to make our communications more streamlined.

The subject line

I cannot emphasize enough the importance of the subject line. In my experience, the subject line can be the most important information on the entire communication. This will help identify the matter and will help with subsequent responses and threads (not to mention when you have to "Find" the matter on a pile of e-mails). To me, the subject line sometimes is the message in itself. The subject line should summarize the content of the message. It is difficult to follow a thread that has as a subject line "New Matter" or something similar. In addition, think about whether the recipient of the message is likely to read it on their mobile device or laptop.

I typically like putting in place some form of protocol for our email subject lines, with a view to making it clear whether action is required. It all depends on your practice, but what I typically like in the subject line of my communications follow a particular order:

- COUNTRY (in capital letters);
- Name/type of matter or project name (see below);
- Deadline (it is very important that any approaching deadlines are included in the subject line); and
- Reference number (if available).

For confidentiality and quick-reference purposes I strongly recommend assigning a project name to your most important matters. I have witnessed too many instances in which the subject line refers to a sensible project (e.g. "Acquisition in Iceland") instead of "Project X". I follow a completely arbitrary naming protocol, but there are many sources and manner of doing it. If you have progressive projects, for example, a simple manner is to follow the Greek alphabet (i.e. Project Alpha, Project Beta, etc.).

In some other instances, your subject line could follow the following principles:

- Urgent – if something requires immediate attention;
- Action – the recipient is required to take some action by a certain date;
- Read – please read this information as you might find it useful (think twice about sending this type of information or set some context as to why the recipient should read the material); and
- Info – passing information on, e.g. organization announcements.

Please note that this practice would be solely with outside counsel, because you will typically receive all e-mails marked as "Urgent" from your internal clients.

"TO" or "CC"?

Within the scope of the "rules of engagement", I advise my outside counsel that it is easier for me to take faster action if I am the direct recipient of a communication; that is, if I appear in the "TO" line. Understandably, if you have others that need to comment on a message, the way I address this is via somehow highlighting/color-coding the name of the person in the body of the message. However, we need to be very selective on who needs to be included in the messages to begin with (including the internal clients, when applicable) and whether those copied, need to take any action.

Follow-ups

Due to the great amount of e-mails I receive on a daily basis, I have two rules of thumb:

1. I do not send acknowledge receipts to messages because I truly believe that they only create more unnecessary communications.
2. I ask outside counsel to follow up with me if they have not received a response within a certain period of time (and with sufficient time if there is a deadline).

I can understand if it may seem contradictory to advise outside counsel that they cannot rely on the fact that, if they sent me an email, I may have read or analyzed it but I simultaneously do not acknowledge receiving the communication in the first place. However, on a day-to-day basis it will all make sense.

So, what is the solution? If something is time-sensitive and important, and you have not received a response, please give me a call on a reasonable schedule.

Start with your conclusion

As mentioned above, I ask my outside counsel to always begin their message with the conclusion: one or two lines that addresses the question presented, followed by risks and alternatives; most importantly, in plain English. You can then expand in the body of the e-mail with more detail. However, in that sense, I strongly prefer the use of bullets, instead of paragraphs.

The ongoing relationship – other considerations when engaging external counsel

More companies are demanding all their service providers (including outside counsel) take into consideration implementing strict compliance programs, as well as diversity and inclusion initiatives (including gender paid equity) and how they encourage personal and professional growth within their organizations.

Corporate social responsibility – diversity and inclusion and gender pay equity

To me Diversity is spelled with a capital "D" because it encompasses a broad definition of people with different backgrounds and experiences, regardless of race, ethnicity, gender, religion, etc. Having diversity and inclusion initiatives generates business benefits and leads to better performance. There are many studies that demonstrate that that diversity in companies help with their bottom line[1] and that certainly includes external counsel. When engaging outside counsel, regardless of where they are located, we should inquire whether they have employee resources groups and D&I programs. Do they have any community outreach or pro bono work? As your outside counsel is the expansion of your team, they must also represent your brand and your values, including aspects of diversity and inclusion.

A current example, and the most evident global advances in this realm, are the efforts to advance gender pay equity. Although there are various examples in the US, there is tremendous increased activity globally. Take, for example, the *Global Gender Gap Report 2018*.

Compliance

It goes without saying that we must all operate with compliance to all local legal requirements. However, in addition, as lawyers, we must cultivate and drive a culture of compliance that, in certain cases, may actually be a higher standard than the local legal requirements.

Driving the compliance culture should be a joint effort between in-house and outside counsel. Some law firms with a global footprint have very well developed compliance programs and they may even have their own code of business conduct (and ethics). However, some smaller boutique law firms may not necessarily have that. As in-house counsel, we should be able to enable that development with them.

These efforts should not be merely establishing a "compliance policy" in writing, but further develop it into the proper training (just like what you have internally). At a minimum, all law firms should have a framework in which all associates fully understand:

1. Conflicts of interest;
2. Anti-corruption and anti-bribery;
3. Travel, entertainment and courtesies;
4. Discrimination and harassment;
5. Privacy and date protection; and
6. Sanctions.

Cultural awareness when engaging outside counsel

One last question I wanted to ask is that, if your company is expanding internationally, how well-prepared are you for the international exposure? When engaging in multiple jurisdictions, we should be aware of the differences as well as the similarities. This exposure will raise legal issues. You will also face other challenges:

- Countries with different economic developments;
- Different cultures;
- Different business practices;
- Different legal systems; and
- Different political systems.

Whilst it is important that your outside counsel keep you up-to-speed with the local laws, at the end of the day – as I have always told the outside counsel I have engaged overseas – they become your eyes and ears on the ground. It is key that they keep you updated of legal and other trends in their geographies.

Suffice to say, if you are working with outside counsel overseas, take into consideration the different time zones. I have seen, too many times, colleagues in Asia are the ones typically accommodating the US EST, which results in very late nights. Consider using the "World Clock Meeting Planner" (it has worked wonders for me).

Conclusion

I cannot reiterate enough how I view outside counsel as a partner and extension of the legal function for my company. At the end of the day, the joint goal is to achieve the business objectives of our common client: the company.

Some key takeaways I would like to summarize as part of this chapter would be:

- Your goal working with external counsel should be to establish a sense of team, creating profitable business for the company (and, by consequence, the law firm);
- I hope that, with the support of legal, the company will continue growing, which will foster the continued support from your external resources;
- Communicate clearly your expectation of receiving extraordinary legal advice in a cost-effective and efficient manner, maintaining the highest ethical standards at all times and with full compliance with legal and ethical requirements (including your own policies);
- Establish "rules of engagement" or "guidelines" that will encompass how you would like to work with your external counsel on a day-to-day basis;
- Aim for the guidelines to be easy to follow;
- Ensure consistent procedures with all your outside counsel (and even other suppliers/vendors);
- Clearly establish who is the primary contact at your company responsible for all matters relating to the engagement with the law firm, and do the same with the external firm;
- The subject line is extremely important in the day-to-day communications with external counsel. It is not acceptable to have

a blank subject line, as you should be able to quickly identify the nature of the correspondence;

- Ask counsel to simplify their e-mails to you, to always incorporate the conclusion at the beginning of the communication, and to include solutions;
- Be open to continuously ask for feedback on finding further efficiencies for the company and the guidelines; and
- If the external counsel requires an urgent response, ask them to give you a call (at no charge).

There is no secret formula to what the best manner of collaboration between internal and external counsel is; in principle, it should take only common sense to build and foster the relationship (but, as I have said many times, common sense is sometimes the least common of the senses). Suffice to say, having an open, honest and frequent dialogue with external counsel is the biggest enabler to that effect. You will build trust and with it an inevitable sense of being part of a team, which translate into increased productivity and effectiveness.

At the end of the day, the relationship between internal and external counsel is a human relationship and, as such, requires nurturing. Take the time, make the effort, and invest to that effect.

Sources

Leading with Cultural Intelligence – David Livermore
The Communication Catalyst – Mickey Connolly and Richard Rianoshek
Building an Outstanding Legal Team – Bjarne Tellmann
Managing the Professional Service Firm – David H Maister
https://www.jdsupra.com/legalnews/voice-of-the-client-10-ways-to-achieve-26942/
https://www.mckinsey.com/business-functions/organization/our-insights/why-diversity-matters
https://www.wonolo.com/blog/50-must-read-articles-on-diversity-in-the-workplace/
https://www.mckinsey.com/~/media/mckinsey/business%20functions/organization/our%20insights/delivering%20through%20diversity/delivering-through-diversity_full-report.ashx
https://lnkd.in/gcYVctX
https://www.intralinks.com/blog/2014/12/whats-ma-project-name

Reference

1. https://www.bcg.com/en-us/publications/2018/how-diverse-leadership-teams-boost-innovation.aspx

Chapter 3:
Leveraging the c-suite – tips for the modern GC

By Ian White, member of Sherwood psf Consulting and former chief legal officer and company secretary

A busy day in the life of the general counsel…

John Renderback III was late. He usually was! It wasn't his fault, of course – it never was! It was that lousy external lawyer he had been using on a major project. Why come to a meeting having not drafted the contract in the way instructed? John had been forced to go through the agreement line by line. It was lucky he had a background in intellectual property, as that was where the main weaknesses were. An hour meeting had turned into three and he was now late for the board meeting. Not for the first time, either – not great given he was the general counsel and corporate secretary. Oh well.

He pushed open the boardroom door of Ark Resourcing Technology Inc. Ten faces looked up, their faces reflected in the shiny mahogany table. "Sorry guys, got tied up with some tedious contract – left it to the externals again; knew I shouldn't. Idiots. Anyway, I'm here now." The CEO, Melissa Mantis, looked up – what was he thinking of, calling her "guy"? She would have to talk to Renderback – again. Why could he never be on time? After all, he was supposed to be taking the minutes and advising the board. This looked bad in front of the chair and the non-executives.

"Okay, John, but try and make sure it doesn't happen again," Donald Butcher, the chair, barked. It certainly wouldn't, Melissa thought to herself. "Sit at the end of the table – we are just about to review the minutes. Anyone have any comments?" "Mr Chair," one of the NEDs usefully contributed, "On page 14, there is a "t" missing from the first word – should be 'stock exchange', not 'sock exchange'." There were wry smiles. John went a shade of red.

The meeting proceeded, John scribbling the minutes. His phone pinged with a text. He looked down – it was that idiot lawyer again – what now?

Some question John had already answered – why didn't the guy get it? A quick text back outlining what needed to be done. The chair's voice: "So John, on the basis that we may have an issue have to reissue the bonds, what is the legal liability of the directors under the offer document?" John was still engrossed in explaining what he thought were the rudimentary elements of software licensing, which he expected his external lawyers to have a basic understanding of. "Err, sorry – what – oh yes, the point is that the liability for death or personal injury is always complex – technically the board could..." "JOHN!" barked Melissa, "We're on the next item – we have already discussed the health and safety issue!" "Oh," a shamefaced general counsel replied. "Never mind, we'll get an external to advise."

As the meeting carried on, John could feel the constant glare of Melissa. At the end of the meeting, just as he was leaving the boardroom, he heard: "In my office – NOW!"

So that's a fictionalised and perhaps exaggerated account of how a general counsel might operate. Of course, it doesn't need to be like this, nor should it be! The general counsel is key advisor to the board, with the potential for a high degree of influence. However, this can only be built over time – the GC is likely to have his or her most important contact with the board when the company is dealing with major matters or in time of crisis. As such, they need the respect and trust of the board and its members; this can take time to develop. How do you build the right degree of trust and develop the requisite credibility? Over what matters – critical ones to the company, reputation, budgets and resources? And how do you work with the principal players on the board – chair, CEO, CFO? What do you do if the relationship goes wrong? What type of support do you need to perform this critical role? Ultimately it is all about good communication and relationships. So here are some of my tips...

It's all about relationships

First, you need to build some allies in the business. The most important is the CEO – without their support you'll never achieve your full potential. CEOs often have a jaundiced view of the GC. If they are on the executive team – not always the case – then they are usually way down the pecking order. To be practical, they are never going to have the power of roles like the head of sales, CFO or even HR Director. And few CEOs come from a background of being a lawyer. This last point should be what you remember. I often hear GCs say: "The trouble is that the CEO just doesn't understand me; she has never taken the trouble to find out what I do." As if the CEO comes in each day and thinks, I really must get to know the GC better! They have other issues to think about – such as profit, cashflow, and shareholder pressure. As I advise these GCs, it is up to you to run and own the relationship with your CEO. You have to make the time and trouble to build and nurture the relationship. You can do this by:

- Building some rapport. Go in and have a casual chat from time to time – not when they are on the phone to an angry chair, of course, but get to know them. Personality is everything and while you don't have to like each other there has to be some respect if the relationship is going to work and you are to survive. Lawyers are glass-half-full people by nature, so you don't want to put on a dour demeanour all the time – no one likes a misery. Equally, I recall a chief legal officer who was always cracking jokes in board meetings. The CEO isn't looking for a comedian in their GC – if they want entertainment, let them go to the theater! Maintain, therefore, the right rapport with your CEO and board.
- While informal chats are good, you still need to ensure that you have regular one-to-ones with your CEO (and other senior officers) so that they know what you and your team to do. This is critical: as one of my CEOs once said to me (he was the most effective CEO I reported to), "You do your job, and I'll do mine – all I ask is no surprises." It is as good a mantra as any for building your influence – after all, a major (negative) surprise on your watch and you may be out of the door the next day.
- Next, you need to understand the psychology of your CEO. Really? Yes! To give you an example, I had a very difficult relationship with one CEO I reported to. I made all the obvious mistakes of not communicating well or building the relationship. It was only when we both had some psychometrics tests done that we realised he was high on power and I was driven by achievement. These characteristics do not always match well, and after I knew this I was able to adjust the relationship for the better.
- Getting the CEO and the rest of the executive team to know what legal does. Of course, this doesn't mean bragging about your successes in an arrogant way, but try and show how you have saved the company money – reduced external spend, for example,

or safeguarded its reputation and that of its senior people. Legal is seen as a cost center, and whilst some lawyers try and turn it into a profit one, that is difficult to achieve in practice. However, evidencing cost savings always goes down well. And if you save the reputation of one of the senior corporate officers, you'll have a friend for life!

Remember: you're not just a lawyer

You may be a lawyer and I am sure you're awfully proud of gaining that qualification – as you should be – but now you're working in business, you're also a business person. Indeed, I often advise young in-house lawyers to see themselves as a business person first and a lawyer second, just as the person sitting next to you may be an accountant by background but is now doing a different role. One of the quickest ways of losing influence is for a lawyer to put a professional divide up based on where they come from. It is the old ivory tower mentality – we are employed by the company but somehow not part of it. If that is how you feel, stay in private practice. People in the business will respect you for who you are in terms of background; they will respect you more if you are one of them, and your influence will be a hundred times greater. One of the best examples I heard of this was the very successful GC of a major blue-chip organisation who was invited to go onto the board of another company as a non-executive director. The company secretary of this latter company was dreading this – another lawyer at the boardroom table contradicting his advice! Sometime later I asked the company secretary how it was working out with the new NED. "Brilliantly," he answered, "you would have never guessed the NED was a lawyer." That might be seen as a compliment when you are a lawyer working in business!

Being a businessperson first and foremost will also help you blend into being a member of the executive team. You will be asked for a contribution greater than just legal – your opinion will be valued across the business (although – and here's a tip – I always tend to avoid questions on finance!), and your sphere of influence and collaboration will grow. That will make it much easier for you to push through the things you want to achieve. You'll have some allies on the team – you are one of them, not just the lawyer in the corner.

Tips and tricks

Some other tips include:

- Prioritise, prioritise, prioritise! In the fictional (it is fictional!) example at the beginning of this chapter, Renderback, the GC, was dealing with a contract when his one and only focus should have been on the board. If you are the corporate secretary as well as the GC, then your greatest priority is always the board. Always. They must come first because they are the leaders of the company and the ones in the spotlight and therefore at the greatest risk. Forget multi-tasking – you can't, and nor can anyone else. I review boards for a living now and the number of directors who take their eye of the ball by being on their phone when they should be listening runs into hundreds. As the corporate secretary, you an officer of the company and you owe it to the directors to give them your undivided attention. If you don't, at the very best your sphere of influence with the board and lower down the company will be severely diminished; at worst, you won't be employed anymore! To ensure that you have the credibility and gravitas that you deserve and need to have to be an influential member of the team, you must show that you are on top of your brief and everything is under control. You need to be the most efficient and effective board attendee!
- Don't ask for too much! If you are seeking to gain resourcing and a budget for your department, then don't ask for too much – at least, not too soon. Establish your credentials and build up your reputation first in some of the ways outlined above, and you'll be on firmer ground. It does mean being an effective manager of people and resources, utilizing any legal panel you have well. However, if you do this effectively you will gain a reputation as an effective manager and one who will only ask for things when really needed. That does mean you really need to plan carefully for what you will require (although we all know budgets are exceeded from time to time) and be an efficient project manager. However, careful planning will also avoid the old mantra of legal just being a cost center.
- The other thing a GC needs to be – at least, if they are influential – is calm. Often the GC is asked to advise when there is a crisis or other difficulty within the company. If they are flapping around in a panic – probably because they are not on top of things and have not

followed some of the pointers in this chapter – their influence and credibility will be shot to pieces. Your internal stakeholders need calm, critical thinking on how to get out of a difficult situation, and the GC is there to help them – that's your role!

- Finally, if you want to be an effective and influential GC, remember you can't do it alone. No one can, not even the best of us. So have a coach – someone completely independent from the organisation – who you can talk to in order to find solutions. A mentor is also beneficial, as there is nothing better than talking with someone who has been there before. These people should help you considerably in your role in dealing with the board, not least because you will have another perspective.

Good luck!

It could have all been so different…

A busy day in the life of the general counsel…

John Renderback III was in the boardroom. It was just dawn. He was two hours early for the board meeting – he always was. He paced up and down the room checking everything was running to order – projector, slides, coffee and tea prepared, lunch fixed. Frankly the trivialities annoyed him but he knew the hassle there would be if coffee was cold or lunch late: it wasn't worth it. John re-read the papers. Third time! He amended his notes on the items he had to talk about, but he could talk on any of the others – even finance.

Melissa Mantis walked in an hour later. Melissa was the CEO – he had worked with her in the past and she had poached him from his previous company. They weren't friends outside of work but there was huge mutual respect – his role was to ensure she was never embarrassed in front of the board, or indeed anyone. And she wasn't. When he had joined Ark Resourcing Technology Inc., she had just said, "You know, John, you're really the only lawyer I have any time for – that's why I hired you. I just ask 'no surprises'." He had followed this mantra ever since. They did a final walkthrough of the papers – "The bond issue is the main thing to be concerned about," John said. "If you lead just bring me in when you think appropriate. I can reassure the board, and I have also taken external advice." "Great," Melissa replied. At that moment his phone pinged – it was an external lawyer advising on a contract. John had little time for him: "Not today, I am in the board meeting. Contact one of my team if you need an answer."

The meeting started on time. John took the minutes – a job he hated, but they were always 100 percent correct, aligned with his 100 percent engagement with the directors and their needs. When it came to the bond issue, the chair expressed his concerns: "What are we going to do – Melissa, John?" John let Melissa speak first; when she brought him in he clearly explained the options. The board felt reassured, and the rest of the meeting progressed well.

As they left the room, he heard Melissa call after him: "John – coffee in my office?"

Chapter 4:
Legal analytics – why do you need it and how do you build it?

By Aaron Katzel, founder and CEO of The Better Legal Infrastructure Project LLC and former head of AIG's legal operations center

> *I often say that when you can measure what you are speaking about, and express it in numbers, you know something about it; but when you cannot express it in numbers, your knowledge is of a meagre and unsatisfactory kind; it may be the beginning of knowledge, but you have scarcely, in your thoughts, advanced to the stage of science, whatever the matter may be.*
>
> William Thomson, Lord Kelvin, May 3, 1883, lecture on "Electrical Units of Measurement" (Popular Lectures and Addresses, Vol. 1, page 73, "Electrical Units of Measurement", 1883).

Why are legal analytics important? If you can't measure it, you can't manage it

The past decade has seen a dramatic rise in the number and sophistication of tools supporting legal analytics.[1] From understanding the sources of legal costs or contract turnaround time, to predicting the behavior of individual lawyers and judges, opportunities for legal analytics have grabbed the attention of attorneys, clients and investors.[2] But why has legal analytics received so much recent attention, and is this the start of a field with lasting importance, or is it merely the latest fad?

In this chapter, we'll examine why legal analytics is important, and why it will almost certainly only grow in significance throughout the legal industry. From there, we'll explore the basics of building a legal analytics program – how to determine which metrics matter to your business or firm, build the right data, process and technology infrastructure to support legal analytics, and set near term and long term goals for your program.[3] Finally, we'll peer into what the future holds for legal analytics – the promise of on-demand predictive legal risk identification, quantification and mitigation, which may arise sooner than many observers expect.

So why should we care about legal analytics? The answer lies in the observation at the start of this chapter, one originally from the field of scientific inquiry, but which has evolved over time into the widely cited business maxim: "If you can't measure it, you can't manage it."

Let's think about this concept for a moment. Regardless of your area of the legal specialty, your work almost certainly includes a set of goals. Some of these goals may be near term, some longer term. Some may apply to work you perform repeatedly, over large volumes; some may apply to large, discrete projects that are unlikely to recur. Lawyers have goals irrespective of whether they work for a law firm or a company's in-house legal function or the government, and no matter what country they work in. Your goals may relate to direct characteristics of the work you perform, such as generating 50 draft purchase agreements each month, or ancillary qualities, such as reducing the costs associated with defending legal claims against your business.

Yet notwithstanding the diversity of these types of goals, they all have one thing in common – they include some definition of what success looks like. And, if success is thoughtfully defined, it's based on a set of metrics that allow you and your boss to measure whether you've achieved your goal (or how far away from achieving it you are, or by what measure you've exceeded it). So these metrics, and the data and analytics that allow you to understand your progress in reaching them, are critical to your success in achieving your goals. They provide the guidance that allow you to correct course, so that you (or the lawyers you manage) can deliver the legal service your client is looking for, when they expect to receive it.

To illustrate the importance of data and analytics in achieving goals, let's look at an example from outside the legal field:

> *Gordon the guided missile sets off in pursuit of its target. It immediately sends out signals to discover if it is on the right course to hit that target. Signals come back: "No, you are not on course. So change it. Up a bit and slightly to the left." And Gordon changes course as instructed and then, rational little fellow that he is, sends out another signal. "Am I on course now?" Back comes the answer, "No, but if you adjust your present course a bit further up and a bit further to the left, you will be." ...And the guided missile goes on and on making mistakes, and on and on listening to feedback and on and on correcting its behavior until it blows up the nasty enemy thing. And we applaud the missile for its skill. If, however, some critic says, "Well, it certainly made a lot of mistakes on the way", we reply, "Yes, but that didn't matter, did it? It got there in the end."*
>
> "The Importance of Mistakes," John Cleese

This amusing example illustrates several different concepts helpful to success in today's legal industry. But for purposes of this chapter, let's focus only on what it tells us about data and analytics. First, in order to achieve his goal – i.e., blowing up the bad guy – Gordon needs a lot of data: information relevant to what he's doing, and what he needs to do in order to achieve his goal. In the example, this data includes information like Gordon's current location, speed, and trajectory, and the location of his target. In the legal space, relevant data may include less lethal characteristics such as which draft contracts are currently at a given stage of the drafting and execution process, or what costs are associated with a particular phase of litigation, or which judge is most likely to find a certain line of legal reasoning persuasive. In all of these examples, the data is the raw information generated by the processes relevant to what we do. However, on its own that information is not terribly useful. Rather, in order to help us achieve our goals, we need to convert the data into reporting or recommendations based on a set of metrics aligned to our goals. That's the function of analytics.

In John Cleese's example, analytics allow Gordon to meet his goal. Throughout his journey, Gordon constantly transmits data, which is compared to other data collected on his target, in order to establish his progress in achieving a metric relevant to his goal: flying at a trajectory and speed that will enable him to land on the bad guy. The signals coming back allow Gordon to course correct throughout his journey so he's more likely to achieve that ultimate goal. All of this is part of a sophisticated system of analytics that gathers data from multiple sources, converts it into a set of relevant metrics, reports back on the progress on those metrics, and repeats the process until the goal is met. While today's legal field lacks the sophisticated systems and algorithms supporting rocket science, legal processes are increasingly measured and analyzed as part of analytics programs designed to improve their performance. And the first step in creating a successful legal analytics program is making some basic decisions about metrics.

Which metrics matter? Deciding what to measure and why

Clients often ask me, "What metrics are important in the legal industry?" By which they mean, "What do I need to track in order to know if I'm doing a good job?" Unfortunately, the honest answer to this question is, "It depends." What does this mean, and why are we left with such an unsatisfying answer?

When I say, "It depends," in response to questions on legal metrics, what I mean is, "The legal metrics important to you depend on your specific goals, and how you plan to achieve them." Because the legal industry is not monolithic. A sprinter and a marathon runner are both runners, yet they have very different goals. "Of course," the clever reader may say, "but ultimately their goal is completing a race." While this is true in a general sense, the characteristics of the races the two very different athletes run, and what a successful outcome looks like, lead to very different definitions of success, and very different metrics on the desirable times for completing 100 meters, 500 meters, or a mile. Similarly, a transactional attorney specializing in mergers and acquisitions has very different goals, and should be measured by very different metrics, from a litigator who defends a company against claims of patent infringement. Indeed, that patent litigator will have very different goals, and will be judged by different metrics, from an employment defense attorney, even though both lawyers are litigators.

So how should legal departments and firms determine what metrics matter as they create a legal analytics program? Although the legal department or the firm as a whole may have one or two overarching goals (e.g., reduce the company's overall legal exposure, increase client revenues), individual lawyers or groups of lawyers will need to be measured differently to ensure they make consistent progress toward making their specific contributions to reaching those goals. This requires looking closely at the processes the different types of attorneys use to deliver their legal work in your department or firm, and understanding what a good outcome of those processes looks like. Although it sounds basic, getting this step right is important, because people in organizations tend to perform their work based on the metrics by which they're being measured, in the hope of ultimately achieving their goals. Poorly defined metrics will almost inevitably lead to bad outcomes because they incentivize the wrong activities. Well-defined metrics tend to resemble Gordon's speed and trajectory – they're supported by a regular stream of reliable data, they encourage performance aligned to the end goal, and they're reported on frequently enough to allow the individual to correct course if it turns out they're not trending to meet their objective.

What are some examples of useful legal metrics? Bearing in mind that every organization's goals and processes will differ, here are a few ideas that could be relevant for a particular business or function:

- Number of error-free draft lease agreements generated and sent for client review each month;
- Number of regulatory requests for additional information in response to a client's antitrust filing;

- Number of days required to fully respond to a client's antitrust regulatory requests for additional information; and
- Total cost associated with completing the discovery phase in defending "slip and fall" cases involving the client's retail facilities;

What makes each of these examples a useful legal metric? They all share a few important qualities: (1) they're defined in a way that supports regular measurement and reporting; (2) they're sufficiently specific to encourage improvement in a key process performed by the lawyer that's aligned to achievement of a larger goal (e.g., improved business productivity, quicker error-free transaction closing, reduced litigation defense cost); and (3) they're not so prescriptive that they prevent the lawyer from experimenting with different approaches to figure out what works best over time. Bad legal metrics, on the other hand, tend to be overly general (or, alternatively, overly prescriptive), vague, unsupported by regular, consistent data and reporting, or aligned to a process that isn't relevant to an important goal of the department or organization. The inevitable consequences of bad legal metrics are inconsistent or undesired outcomes, friction between managers and employees, and low morale.

Where does your information come from, is it scalable and reliable, and how do you make it usable?

As we've seen, in devising the right legal metrics for your department or firm, you'll inevitably start to get a better understanding of your organization's legal processes and data infrastructure. Why? Well, these three areas are inextricably linked, and make up the foundations of a successful legal analytics program. When set up properly, the processes by which a company or firm obtains or delivers its legal services regularly generate data that's captured in a consistent way by systems, and which can be converted into the metrics that a mature legal analytics program reports on.

To return to John Cleese's example, the rocket scientists who designed the analytics underpinning Gordon's navigation weren't concerned about creating a different process or set of metrics for each of the many different bad guys Gordon may be pointed at, or the weather conditions, or even Gordon's launch site. Instead, they developed a set of metrics (trajectory, location and speed) with respect to which data could be captured and reported on regularly, and which would give Gordon the right feedback needed to correct course in achieving his ultimate goal. Unfortunately, yet all too frequently, law firms and companies' legal departments have grown and evolved in one or more ways that present obstacles to the creation of mature legal analytics programs.

What are some of these obstacles, and why do they emerge? In my experience, two of the most common challenges in building successful legal analytics include:

- A lack of understanding of the critical processes underlying how legal services are consumed or delivered by the organization; and
- Failing to capture data from the legal group's key processes, or to capture it in a consistent way.

Let's address these challenges. In large part due to our training and the history of our profession, lawyers often don't think about their services in a process-oriented way. What do I mean by this? Well, to consider a few examples, we lawyers tend not to realize that we undertake certain steps regularly in completing a particular type of transaction or supporting the litigation of a particular legal claim. Instead, we're trained to perceive the *differences*, rather than the characteristics that are broadly similar, across the work we typically do. So we look at each matter as highly bespoke or artisanal, requiring individualized attention, analysis and planning. And, as a result, the systems supporting lawyers frequently haven't been designed in a way that's aligned to the common processes we use to successfully deliver our legal services. And because they haven't been designed to align to those processes, those systems often don't capture the data (or don't capture it consistently) that show critical characteristics in how those legal processes are performed.

As a result, many businesses or firms looking to build a legal analytics program need to invest significant time and effort on the basic "blocking and tackling" work involved in understanding:

- What are the critical processes that underlie delivery of the legal services relevant for the group's goals?
- What systems support those processes?
- What data is captured by those systems?
- How is the data defined (e.g., what elements are included, and what are excluded, when we collect data on "legal costs," and are those elements defined in the same way)?
- What risks threaten the regular, reliable generation of that data (e.g., is the data automatically captured by a system tied to the

process involved, or is it entered manually by different people who may interpret the requirements differently)?

And, once they have these understandings, they'll need to invest time and effort to configure their systems in a way that generates consistent, reliable data on the performance of their key legal processes. Often this step involves the legal department partnering with experts in data architecture, statistics, and IT systems who will ensure the group's process and IT infrastructure supports an acceptable level of data integrity. The "cleaned up" data, in turn, comprises the raw material that supports reliable, regular reporting on the legal metrics critical to any successful legal analytics program. Legal departments or firms hoping to avoid, or looking to take shortcuts on, these critical foundational steps will quickly experience the embarrassment and loss of credibility associated with another well-worn business maxim: "Garbage in, garbage out."

Moving up the maturity ladder – growing from reporting to self-service analytics

As we've seen, building a successful legal analytics program involves time and effort. This doesn't mean that you need to wait years before seeing results. Instead, I recommend setting near-term and longer-term institutional goals for your program, as part of a comprehensive analytics strategy. This will allow you to reap the benefits of improved operating and financial performance, even as the sophistication of your legal analytics improves over time.

What might these different goals look like? Let's work back from an end state "legal analytics nirvana." This could involve interactive dashboards easily accessible from every laptop in the legal department, which allow the user to check daily (based on automatically updated data) on the progress he or she (or his or her team) has made toward their goals based on the metrics relevant to their performance. The dashboard could even project the likelihood of achievement of their annual goals, based on their current performance (adjusted perhaps, for known variables like expected cost variations based on the jurisdiction and phase of litigation pending on the attorney's docket). Building a sophisticated platform like this is an effort that will take years for most legal departments, under an extended project involving professionals with diverse skills and many interim steps. Although this may sound daunting, it's not impossible, and companies willing to undertake the necessary discipline and commit the right resources and investment have successfully evolved their legal analytics capabilities from unreliable, labor-intensive, manual reporting to sophisticated, automated, self-reporting systems such as these.

If self-service, individualized analytics is an aspirational long-term goal, what does a good interim result look like? Frequently, this involves a manually generated set of reports on a few important metrics designed to drive critical goals. The reports will be prepared and circulated based on a prescribed calendar, perhaps quarterly or bi-monthly, designed to support the legal team's ability to measure their performance against those metrics, and allow them to adjust course if necessary to meet their goals. Over time, the process for generating the reports should become more automated, and the metrics reported on may become more sophisticated. Throughout this process, in order to maintain reliability, careful attention must be paid to ensuring that there's a well-documented, thorough understanding of how the data supporting legal analytics is generated, how it's defined, and how it's converted into reporting on the relevant metrics.

What does the future hold? Legal risk identification, quantification and mitigation: predictive legal analytics

The sophistication of legal analytics tools is rapidly evolving. Leveraging advances in computing power, machine learning and other forms of "artificial intelligence," and the growth in available data, technology changing how lawyers work in fundamental ways is becoming widely accessible.[4] This includes tools allowing lawyers to make more informed settlement decisions in light of the likely outcomes of their litigation, based on the type of claim, judge involved, and identity of opposing counsel. Other advances include systems that will automatically alert companies to potential legal and compliance risks, based on continuous computerized review of numerous sources of data generated by a company's manufacturing, sales, treasury and communications processes and systems. Some of these applications will use data generated by the activities of the law department or firm using the platform. Others will analyze data from public sources, such as courts, government agencies and public records. Many will generate recommendations or solutions based on both internal and public sources of information. While many of these tools will make access to sophisticated analytics dramatically easier and cheaper than today, a few of the fundamental principles discussed in this chapter are unlikely to change.

First, any tool is only useful to the extent it helps you achieve your specific goals. The world's best screwdriver isn't terribly helpful if you need to remove a nail. It's not uncommon that we're so dazzled by the latest advances in technology that we forget to consider that often a simpler, proven, less costly tool may better help us achieve our objectives. Second, no advance in technology is likely to cure the "garbage in, garbage out" problem. Any analytics tool is only as good as the data it processes. So if your data is unreliable, inconsistent, or generated by poorly regulated processes and sources, even the most sophisticated analytics platform will provide unreliable, inconsistent reporting, recommendations or conclusions at best. As a result, every legal department and law firm looking to achieve better outcomes based on analytics using their own data will be well served by investing time and effort in creating a robust, well-regulated legal data infrastructure.

Better legal outcomes. Lower costs. Reduced compliance risk and legal exposure. More engaged, productive legal professionals. All of these goals can be achieved by leveraging today's legal analytics tools. Savvy legal departments and law firms that take the time and effort to understand their processes, create a well-regulated data environment, and select metrics and analytics tools designed to advance their goals, will discover that legal analytics can deliver benefits for years to come.

References

1. The In-House Counsel's Legal Tech Buyer's Guide, {LawGeex} 2018.
2. *Ibid*, observing that, "The global legal analytics market, valued at $450 million in 2017, is expected to reach $1.8 billion by 2022."
3. One topic outside the scope of this chapter is the legal and compliance review required to create a successful legal analytics program. It is of course critical to understand, and create a compliant environment addressing, the implications of your legal analytics program on attorney-client confidentiality and privilege, data privacy and information security requirements, and other applicable laws and regulations. Unfortunately space limitations prevent adequate discussion of these topics, which are covered elsewhere at length.
4. Indeed, early or limited versions of some of the technologies discussed in this section are already available.

Chapter 5:
Three key steps to drive change through innovative contracting

By Peggy Chang Barber, Americas CEO and general counsel for The International Association for Contract and Commercial Management

In today's competitive environment, general counsels are under increasing pressure to make contracting simpler, faster and better aligned with digital business. These challenging times provide fantastic opportunities for innovation, and Speed to Contract (S2C) is an innovation that offers tremendous value for both customers and suppliers. The faster the parties come to "yes," the sooner critical solutions can drive a customer's business success, the quicker involved personnel can shift to other tasks, and the earlier revenue streams can hit the supplier's books.

However, contracts in agile times are often considered to be a nuisance, a necessary evil and appreciated only by lawyers. Tesla CEO Elon Musk went as far as saying in July of 2018 that his company wants to eliminate all of its customer contracts, tweeting that: "We're trying to get rid of contracts completely. Should just be 'tap here & you get your car'. Then, if you don't like it for any reason, just return it like any other product." While some may lament the current state of affairs, many forward-leaning general counsels are taking a fresh look at how they approach contracting and making changes to transform the role of the legal function in the contracting process.

You might ask why contracting and S2C have become key focus areas for legal departments when general counsels are bombarded with such a wide range of issues and challenges. In 2016, as part of awarding the Nobel Prize in Economic Science to Oliver Hart and Bengt Holmstrom for their thought-leading work in contract design and outcome optimization, the Royal Swedish Academy of Sciences observed that "...modern economies are held together by innumerable contracts... and since such relationships typically entail conflicts of interest, contracts must be properly designed to ensure that the parties take mutually beneficial decisions." Yet today, trade relationships are increasingly fractured and threatened because of a steady decline of trust.

Rather than designing for mutual benefit, contracts are more often used as instruments of power and control. Research by The International Association for Contract and Commercial Management (IACCM), a global non-profit professional association dedicated to raising the quality and integrity of trading relationship, indicates that contract terms are often penal in nature – we contract for the divorce rather than the marriage – and they are complicated to understand. They often reflect commercial policies and practices that are defensive and risk-averse in nature, even though market and economic conditions demand different approaches which are flexible, adaptive, creative and outcome-based. In addition, IACCM benchmarking reports show that many organizations do not have a well-defined, end-to-end contracting process. Frequently, contract and commercial activities are sub-elements in other processes – for example, in product lifecycle management, procurement, project management or sales operations. Tasks are therefore often "functionalized", leading to a lack of cohesion and poor data flows across multiple groups and systems.

Ultimately, it means that, in many organizations, no one has an overview of who is responsible for producing a complete contract, whether that contract is "fit for purpose", nor how well individual contracts or the contracting process are performing. To achieve S2C, contracting must be viewed as a team sport, involving multiple stakeholders within and outside of the business. However, contracting is often mistakenly seen solely as the responsibility of in-house legal departments, and that view can be challenging for general counsels when they are asked by their CEOs to lead transformation.

While inefficiencies associated with contracting are difficult to overcome by any function – particularly one not responsible for their outcomes, like the legal department – there is no higher compliment than to be asked to solve a problem so strategically important to the business. Opportunities for transformation abound, and most of them do not require a huge budget and new technology to implement. What they do require, however, is an acknowledgement of contracting as a discipline, a field of study and not just a function. It also takes a willingness to learn, to look outside of the organization for external perspective or "outsights", and to be open to new ways of thinking to achieve contracting excellence.

The concept of contracting as a discipline is a critical mindset change for legal departments who want to drive innovative change. Most legal departments are comprised of those who have gone through legal training and those who have been trained in other disciplines. Just because someone has gone through legal training does not in and of itself make the person an expert in contracting. In trading relationships, the issues that arise are often not about whether what the parties want to do is legal or illegal. The discussions are about what makes the most business sense for the parties. Those who lead contract drafting, negotiation and management – whether legally trained or not – need to understand the business and the end-to-end contracting process, to keep updated on the latest research, outsights and innovations in the contracting discipline, and to develop the collaborative mindset that enables innovative thinking. Attending continuing legal education is simply not enough.

Transformational opportunities

With that said, given the importance of contracts in delivering business results, what steps can a general counsel reasonable initiate? Let's look at three transformational opportunities that most legal departments should be able to implement without significant budget or technology investments.

1. Streamlining or (better yet!) eliminating routine negotiations

Do you often feel that you are negotiating the same issues over and over, with similar results? In most buy-sell arrangements, we know where negotiation over issues like ownership, audit, confidentiality, privacy and liability will likely end. Yet each party usually starts with a position that favors them, and time is wasted posturing instead of addressing deal specific issues with real business impact and expediting S2C to deliver much needed business solutions and revenue to the parties.

Why not start where we know we will end, and rewrite contract templates and guidelines so the opening position or response you provide is fair and reasonable for the parties? Since legal departments often own or manage templates, clause libraries and negotiation guides, they are perfectly placed to consider issues that are most frequently negotiated and whether it makes sense to streamline or eliminate negotiation altogether without materially increasing risk. Elimination of negotiation empowers the business and drives the concept of automated or "no touch" contracting, which we see with increasing frequency for non-disclosure agreements.

To get started, you can get a good sense of your most frequently negotiated issues and where they close by: (1) surveying your contract negotiation experts; and (2) analyzing your executed agreements versus your standard positions. Hopefully the results from (1) and (2) are fairly close. You can also gather publicly available templates posted on your competitors' websites and compare them against your template to get a sense of whether your starting positions are market competitive.

With both an internal view and a market view, you have the data you need to determine whether it makes sense to modify your starting position to a fair or perhaps even a "better than market" position to obtain a competitive advantage. This work can be done manually or through the use of automation, leveraging organizations like IACCM who have access to benchmarking data and tools to expedite your journey in a cost effective way.

You can also or instead consider adopting the approach taken by the IACCM Contracting Principles.[1] These principles incorporate feedback from over 200 organizations across industries and geographies on six key issues to start (ownership, liability, indemnity, service level agreements, audit and privacy/data security), with more to come, and they offer contracting parties the ability to take fair and balanced positions at the start of negotiations on contracting terms that frequently absorb significant time and resource.

2. Implementing contract simplification and visualization

After over 20 years of being a lawyer, I still see contract terms that make no sense and clients who disregard contracts because they are too complicated to understand. I was fascinated, therefore, by the story of Robert de Rooy, a commercial attorney in South Africa who created a comic contract as "a way for illiterate people to independently understand contracts, use that understanding to guide their behavior, and improve the relationships between contracting parties." Replacing a lengthy, wordy and highly legalistic contract with a document comprised of simple language and pictures, Rob's comic contracts made it possible for fruit pickers with limited literacy to understand their job requirements, leading to a much more productive relationship between employer and employees.

Using pictures to drive clarity is not a new concept. For example, artist Candy Chang collaborated with The Street Vendor Project and the Center for Urban Pedagogy in 2009 to create the street vendor guide for New York City when it became clear that street vendors did not understand the many rules and regulations promulgated by the city. Translating this concept to contracts? Now that's innovation!

Imagine having contracts that the business clients understand and are excited to use to manage trade relationships to successful conclusion. Think about the positive impact to ease of doing business, time to revenue and business outcomes. Again, legal departments are perfectly placed to drive this change, because contract templates are usually owned or managed by the legal department in most corporations.

For ideas on how to get started, consider the approach taken by Royal Dutch Shell. Inspired by Robert de Rooy's comic contract, the Shell legal team decided to embark on a journey to transform Shell's standard templates into visual contracts, starting with a pilot in its Marine International division. They engaged IACCM on the effort, and their clients loved the results. Shell created a video describing the process they went through to create visual contracts and the benefits realized so far.[2] The video contains many examples of turning complex contract language into simplified language that will hopefully spark ideas for getting started on your own simplification and visualization journey.

To take this effort a step further and drive true competitive advantage, consider whether your contract templates and approach align with your brand, your business value and the commitment you intend to make in your trading relationships. In his May 3, 2019 blog, Tim Cummins – president and founder of IACCM – points out that, for many organizations, there is a significant difference between public and marketing statements and commitments in contracts, and he makes the following case for aligning contracts with brand and value: "Is it really the case that contracts should be about minimizing commitments or – far worse – trying to take advantage of people, of suppliers, of customers? Is that the standard of ethical behavior to which you and your business aspire? If not, then it's time to undertake an evaluation, to bring your contracts into line with your value system – and perhaps to make them something that is designed for users, a source of pride, a communication that can be understood."[3]

3. Getting educated on contracting and commercial management

In most legal departments, lawyers lead negotiation of the most complex transactions and handle the most challenging post-contract disputes, but they are often not steeped in the business, the contracting process or the latest in contracting research, benchmarking, innovations and outsights. Many treat negotiations like a battle rather than a collaborative effort to achieve a common goal, and they create or perpetuate contract language difficult for most people to understand. They negotiate based on their own experiences, and since most lawyers don't get involved in the day-to-day management of the contracts they negotiate or know the latest in contracting innovations, their experiences have limited relevance when it comes to driving contracting excellence.

That said, most contracts eventually get done, even if the process is painful, and legal departments typically pay for continuing legal

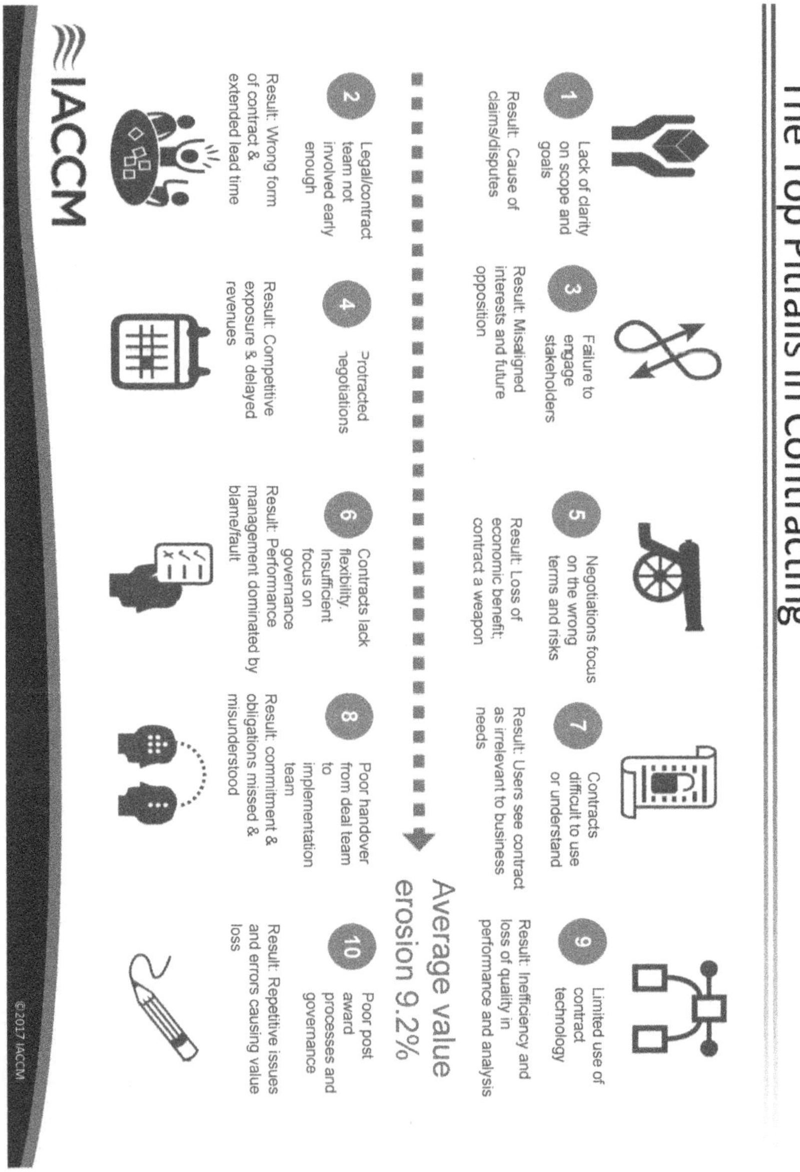

Figure 1: IACCM 10 Contracting Pitfalls

education and some legal conference attendance for their lawyers already. So, why should general counsels consider having their lawyers certified in contracting and commercial management and attend contracting-specific conferences and webinars?

In 2015, IACCM published an eye-opening report on the Ten Pitfalls to Avoid in Contracting[4] and concluded that organizations could generate over nine percent improvement to their bottom line on average if they tackled commercial issues that commonly undermine contract performance. Consider the possibility of adding over nine percent to the bottom line! The ten pitfalls identified in the report and summarized in the graphic below are all issues with contracting strategy, process and approach, not with traditional legal issues and risk.

As general counsels continue to be tapped to driving transformational change in contracting, all members of the legal department who handle contracts, including attorneys, need to do their part, especially when the resulting benefit could be the addition of over nine percent to the bottom line. It is interesting to note that many organizations now have attorneys in contracting roles, and those attorneys are often being trained and certified in contracting and commercial management, while attorneys in formal attorney roles aren't usually considered for such training and certification. The reason given is that those in attorney roles already take continuing legal education. The reality is that continuing legal education does not focus on contracting and commercial management. Neither do most legal conferences.

Also, as contracting is a team sport, stakeholders within and outside of legal in the contracting process also need to be educated on their role in the process. Consider the following questions. Without this article, how would your team members and stakeholders learn the latest in contracting innovations like comic contracts, contracting visualization and the IACCM Contracting Principles? Is your organization at a competitive disadvantage by not focusing on increasing outsights and commercial capabilities of all those who handle contracts or need to contribute to the contracting process?

I promised at the outset to suggest transformations that can be implemented without significant budget or technology investments. Below are some best practices to consider from leading global companies on driving increased commercial capabilities within their organization.

- Join a professional contracting association like IACCM where your team members and stakeholders can attend webinars, exchange ideas with other professionals who are passionate about contracting excellence, learn about their role in the contracting process, and be certified in contracting and commercial management;

- Offer training, certification and conference attendance as a perk for top performers; and
- Incorporate training, certification and the need to bring outsights into job descriptions for significant roles in the contracting process to emphasize contracting as a discipline as well as the need for leaders to continue learning and sharing best practices and innovations from outside of their organization.

Now is the time

As the business environment continues to be more competitive and agile, general counsel will continue to be asked to make contracting simpler, faster and more useful. Now is the time to drive meaningful change that not only transforms ease of doing business, but also firmly establishes the legal function as a team player and an enabler of S2C. I hope the suggestions in this article will assist you in achieving the above and also redefining the legal function as innovators and facilitators of business transformation.

References

1. https://journal.iaccm.com/contracting-excellence-journal/iaccm-contracting-principles.
2. https://www.youtube.com/watch?v=A6Nauutlr1I&feature=youtu.be.
3. https://blog.iaccm.com/commitment-matters-tim-cummins-blog/are-comic-contracts-a-joke
4. https://blog.iaccm.com/free-resources/ten-pitfalls-to-avoid-in-contracting

Chapter 6: Empowering the legal department through Agile methodology

By John E Grant, founder of the Agile Attorney Network

David Graham first jumped into the world of Agile by a happy accident. While serving as in-house counsel and a leader of the Real Estate & Lease Administration team for shoe retailer DSW in 2014, his group recognized the need to replace their aging lease lifecycle management software. Working with technology partners, they settled on a complex solution integrating two SaaS products with considerable custom development.

Although he'd worked on plenty of projects before, Graham had never been part of one quite like this. Instead of giant GANTT charts showing dependencies and milestones, the development team was using sticky notes moving through columns on a board. Instead of lengthy planning and status meetings, the team met frequently for quick check-ins. And instead of long delivery timelines, they were building and testing features block-by-block, so that each iteration built upon their previous work.

The team was using a relatively new methodology known as Agile – specifically a version of Agile called Scrum – to manage and deliver the project. Upon learning how the method worked and seeing how it helped work flow through its various stages of development, Graham was hooked.

"I enjoy the legal work for sure – but legal service delivery these days offers challenges in workflow architecture and oversight as much as lawyering," Graham says. He liked, on the technology project, how the visibility of both the work and the workflow made the process apparent to the team and made oversight more straightforward.

Soon he was applying what he'd learned on that technology project to re-design his team's lease-negotiation workflows. In less than a year of process improvement work they'd shaved weeks off of their negotiation timeline, decreased the lawyer time needed for review, and increased quality – and therefore leverage – by escalating issues earlier in the negotiation. As a result, DSW signed measurably better leases more predictably, and at lower cost.

A brief history of Agile

Agile as a comprehensive methodology is fairly new. Although many concepts that are now considered Agile pre-date the term, we can trace the unified theory to a gathering of software developers and technology managers in early 2001. Frustrated by traditional methods for managing software projects, they gathered in Snowbird, Utah to adopt a "Manifesto for Agile Software Development:"[1]

> *We are uncovering better ways of developing software by doing it and helping others do it. Through this work we have come to value:*
>
> - ***Individuals and interactions** over processes and tools;*
> - ***Working software** over comprehensive documentation;*
> - ***Customer collaboration** over contract negotiation;*
> - ***Responding to change** over following a plan.*
>
> *That is, while there is value in the items on the right, we value the items on the left more.*

Agile adoption spread rapidly in the tech sector and is gaining traction in other business settings. By 2016, 94 percent of respondents to the annual State of Agile Survey[2] reported using Agile in their enterprise. Those companies credit Agile for improvements in their:

- Ability to manage changing priorities (88 percent of respondents);
- Project visibility (83 percent);
- Team productivity (83 percent);
- Delivery speed (81 percent); and
- Team morale (81 percent).

The cover story of the May 2018 *Harvard Business Review* highlights how Agile has spread throughout the enterprise to areas such as "product development, marketing, and even HR."[3] And a 2016 *Lexpert* magazine article highlights successful Agile implementations in law firms and corporate legal teams.[4]

Today, there are a number of specific methodologies that fall under the Agile umbrella. Some are primarily software and technology focused;

examples include eXtreme Programming, Crystal, and DevOps. Others – like Scrum, Kanban, their hybrid ScrumBan, and the Scaled Agile Framework (SAFe – are often used throughout an organization.

Agile for legal

I first became interested in applying Agile methods in a legal setting shortly after earning my J.D. in 2007. Before law school I spent nearly a decade in the technology sector, most of that with a single company, Getty Images. Over that time I participated in a number of technology projects, all of them using what we now think of as traditional, or waterfall, project management techniques.

My first legal job was back at Getty as in-house counsel, working with many of the same teams and people I knew well. While I was away studying, however, Getty's technology managers had shifted to Agile management methods. I'd been vaguely aware of Agile prior to then (my wife works in technology), but being back at Getty was the first time I'd seen it in action. I quickly recognized one thing: it was better.

It wasn't perfect, of course, but the teams were delivering their projects more quickly and with less back-and-forth among constituents (who also seemed to get along better). It yielded results, too: Getty at the time was responding to the rise of social image sharing and a corresponding shift in the photography marketplace. Agile development helped the company to adapt its strategies and stay ahead of shifting customer expectations.

When I transitioned to private practice, I experimented with Agile methods in my own IP boutique. Eventually I began to teach it to other legal professionals informally, then professionally. In the process, I've learned how to translate and adapt Agile concepts so they work well for legal teams.

Today I've taught Agile – plus complementary management methods like Lean, Jobs To Be Done, Lean Startup, and Design Thinking – to thousands of legal professionals on teams of all types and sizes. Over the course of my work, and of observing Agile's evolution in other industries, I've come to recognize four core principles for an Agile legal practice:

- Empower people;
- Define and measure quality;
- Validate assumptions through experimentation;
- Deliver better value yesterday than today.

I'll discuss each of them briefly in turn.

Empower people

Agile has always placed a premium on encouraging people to work together to solve problems and giving them the resources they need to be effective. Nearly every human endeavor involves coordinating a combination of people, processes, and tools to accomplish some goal, and – like Lean and other methods it draws from – Agile recognizes that people are at the heart of that equation.

This is especially true in knowledge work, where creative problem-solving generally outperforms mechanistic labor. Therefore, an Agile legal team will strive to recruit and retain motivated[5] individuals, create a safe environment[6] for creative problem-solving, and empower them with the right processes and tools to be effective.

Define and measure quality

Long before Agile coalesced as a philosophy, great thinkers in the worlds of Lean and Systems Thinking came to a profound conclusion: quality improvement and process improvement are the same thing.[7] In other words, by focusing primarily on delivering quality work to your customer – and understanding how to measure your output against that quality standard – you empower your team to orient its processes and tools around that goal.

This, in turn, helps the team recognize, and reduce or eliminate, activity that does not contribute to its delivery of quality work. In Lean, that extraneous activity is the definition of "waste."[8]

Efficiency on its own is like a shooting star: it's hard to find by focusing intently on it. Instead, the recipe for finding efficiency in knowledge work goes something like this:

- First, seek to understand what constitutes **quality** work (or a quality outcome), usually from your customer's[9] perspective;
- Establish a high-level, documented **standards** that capture the definition of quality and allows measurement against that definition;
- This allows team members to achieve **consistency** in their delivery of quality work, which also helps with **load-balancing** of work among team members;
- Consistent delivery and balanced loads create **capacity** within the team – the ability to accomplish more with the resources you have, which in turn yields increased **flow**, or velocity at which the team delivers quality work; and

- **Efficiency** is the result: quality work that is delivered quickly and consistently without unnecessary materials or processing.

Figure 1: How quality improvements yield efficiency

Validate assumptions through experimentation

We've all heard that the only constant is change, and we feel the pace of change accelerating. Futurist Kevin Kelly, founding editor of *Wired* magazine, identifies our era as one of "becoming:" constant evolution into something new. The result, he says, is that our assumptions about the world will require frequent re-evaluation. "In this era of 'becoming,'" he says, "everyone becomes a newbie. Worse, we will be newbies forever. That should keep us humble."[10]

The practice of validating assumptions is a core theme of the Lean Startup method of business and product development. Eric Reis's book[11] by that name incorporates concepts from Lean, Agile, and the scientific method to argue that the knowledge generated from setting goals and measuring progress against them is every bit as important – in some cases more so – than the results of the effort itself. He calls this process "validated learning."

Validated learning requires application of the Deming Cycle,[12] sometimes referred to by one of several initialisms: BML (Build, Measure, Learn), PDCA (Plan, Do, Check, Act), or – my preferred one – PDSA (Plan, Do, Study, Adjust). Too often we proceed to the next project or initiative without conducting the learning components that Deming propounds. In Agile, we capture learning through an after-action-review-style tool called the Retrospective.

Deliver better value yesterday than today

This principle incorporates the Lean concept of Kaizen, or "continuous improvement." It recognizes that small, incremental efforts to improve products, services, or workflows will almost always outperform large-scale initiatives.

Focusing on incremental improvement yields three important benefits. First is the snowball effect: when the improvement effort is successful, we've established a new baseline to improve against. Small improvements over time will compound like interest, building to big results.

Even when the improvement effort fails to yield the intended results, however, by working on small goals with short timelines we limit the investment we make and limit our losses. And by evaluating our incremental efforts, we give ourselves frequent opportunity to adjust. Contrast this with long-term efforts where early misses can throw the project's cost and/or timeline wildly off course.

Whether or not they meet their stated objective, short-term efforts (or experiments) accelerate validated learning. By working with compact timelines and scope, we quickly gain useful information about what works and what doesn't. We can incorporate that validated knowledge into the next small iteration to improve its likelihood of success. In that way, the organization learns how to learn, and improves its core competencies accordingly.

Project management and process improvement in one

Although Agile is often thought of as a project management paradigm, all Agile methods place an emphasis on process improvement as well. Different methods strike a different balance.

Scrum is one of the most widely used methods and is very project management focused. It excels at helping teams build new things – whether a new software product or a new legal case – by aggressively prioritizing requested features, decomposing work into bite-sized pieces, and delivering those pieces in iterative development cycles called sprints. Scrum generally reserves its process improvement component for the end of each sprint using a retrospective.[13]

Kanban,[14] probably the next most common toolset, more thoroughly incorporates process improvement throughout its cycles. Kanban shines as a tool for teams that regularly deliver similar types of work (even when some features vary): deal review workflows, routine document drafting, and even simple litigation. It uses tools that make the work and workflow visible, allowing the team to see where process bottlenecks are forming and work on making improvements.

In my experience, these two methods – along with the hybrid ScrumBan[15] – are best suited to legal workflows. I tend to favor Scrum when there are a significant number of unknown unknowns, and I like Kanban for much of the routine work that lands with in-house teams.

The kanban board

One thing Scrum and Kanban have in common is its use of a kanban board for visualizing the work and workflow. One of the problems with knowledge work is that it is largely invisible, residing either in the innards of our electronic devices or our skulls. Although we humans are certainly capable of holding complex concepts and processes in our heads, it is mentally taxing to do so.

We can try to describe those concepts and processes in words – via things like standard operating procedures or work breakdown structures – but even in a profession devoted to verbal communication it can be challenging to express complex concepts simply. Nobel laureate Daniel Kahneman[16] addresses this in his book *Thinking Fast and Slow*[17] where he distinguishes between System 1 (intuitive) and System 2 (analytical) thinking. Written and spoken communication is primarily analytical, which requires substantial brain resources for formulation and understanding. Visuals, on the other hand, are primarily intuitive, which requires far less brainpower to comprehend.

With that background, we can think of a kanban board as a "visual fiction" for representing knowledge work. We know that the representations on the board are not the work itself, but our brains accept the avatars as truth. By creating true-enough representations of our work and the process for delivering it, we gain a better understanding of the entire system.

Those representations typically have two components. The kanban board itself is divided into columns, with the most basic structure consisting of three: To-do, Doing, and Done. These can be drawn with two lines on a whiteboard, or two strips of painter's tape on a wall. Individual tasks are represented by writing them on cards (often sticky notes) and placing them on the board. Higher-priority tasks go towards the top of the relevant column.

This most basic board structure might resemble a to-do list, but with two important differences. First, the items on a written checklist have only two possible states: done, or not done. By introducing the "doing" column, we now have a representation of work that is in-progress; something that has been started but is not yet complete. That work-in-progress, or WIP[18] is often the silent killer of productivity.[19]

The other advantage of a kanban board is the ease with which tasks can be prioritized and contextualized. With a written checklist, once the list is made it can be difficult to reprioritize items without re-writing the list (stars and highlights only get you so far).[20] With cards on a kanban board, it is simple to reposition tasks to reflect new information that changes priorities.

From that simple three-column board, you can expand the columns to best reflect the needs of the team using it. Many teams expand the "To-Do" column to the left to approximate a funnel of work: e.g. "Today," Tomorrow," "This Week," "This Month." This is a useful approach when teams must prioritize multiple types of work or manage inputs from diverse sources.

Other teams will expand the "Doing" column to reflect multiple stages of work. You can add horizontal swim lanes to represent different types of work, or even a "fire lane" to prioritize emergencies. The permutations are endless, and I encourage teams to experiment to find board structures that meet their needs.

Getting started with your team

At the risk of sounding self-serving, seeking the help of an experienced Agile coach or professional can significantly accelerate your and your team's learning about Agile methods. Engaging an outside consultant, however, isn't the only way to get started. Many organizations have project managers or others in the enterprise who will be familiar with Agile methods and can help educate legal team leaders. Even so, there are several ways to ramp-up and experiment with Agile on your own.

Self-study

Books, of course, are a great resource as well. In addition to the several I've already mentioned, I recommend the following to help give people a better sense of various Agile concepts. Note that none of them is legal-specific, but there is plenty to learn from each.

- *The Phoenix Project* by Gene Kim, Kevin Behr, and George Spafford. This business novel about an IT manager might seem like an odd first choice, but it is one of the best books I've read for engaging people with core concepts from Agile and Lean thinking in a relatable way. The storytelling isn't half bad either, which makes it easy to keep with the book.
- *Scrum: The Art of Doing Twice the Work in Half the Time* by Jeff Sutherland and JJ Sutherland. Jeff Sutherland is one of the

co-creators of the Scrum methodology and an original signer of the Agile Manifesto. While some parts of this book are a little self-congratulatory, it does a good job introducing the basics of Scrum. It contains plenty of specific business cases where Scrum has helped teams succeed, many of which are outside of technology fields.

- *Making Work Visible: Exposing Time Theft to Optimize Work and Flow* by Dominica Degrandis. I can't say enough good things about this book. Degrandis is a technology veteran with a deep understanding of human dynamics in a work setting. Despite cataloging many of the lesser human instincts that rob us of our productivity, the book itself is optimistic and bright. It is full of helpful (and colorful) illustrations and battle-tested advice for getting your work to flow more smoothly.

Kanban for personal productivity

One of the best ways to get a feel for an Agile methodology is to try Kanban for a day. It takes less than five minutes to set up and will help you start learning some of the benefits of Agile methods. The steps are simple, and as you take them keep in mind one of the unofficial slogans of the Kanban method: "Start less to finish more."

1. Find a patch of empty wall or clean off a corner of your white board. You don't need more than a couple of feet square to begin with.
2. Create three columns by drawing two vertical lines on your white board. On a wall you can use painter's tape or, if you don't have any handy, just make column headings with sticky-notes and imagine the lines (remember, this is a prototype – don't over think it).
3. Label the columns from left to right, "To-Do," Doing," and "Done!" (I think the exclamation point is a helpful touch).
4. Grab a pack of sticky notes and write down the tasks you reasonably hope to accomplish that day, one task per sticky. If you think of tasks you don't think you'll get done today you can write them down too, but they'll hang out on your wall to the left of your board for now.
5. Put your most important task at the top of your "To Do" column, with the next most important task immediately below it, and so on. It is important that the cards form a single vertical column.

6. To get started, pull the top card from "To Do," and put it in "Doing."
7. This is the hard part: Don't start on other tasks until you have completed that highest priority item. Once that item is finished, pull it into the "Done!" column to create room for the next-most-important task to flow into "Doing."
8. Repeat until all of your tasks are finished, or you run out of time in the day (hint: it will almost certainly be the latter).

The steps are simple, but you'll likely find execution harder than you think. For one, single-tasking can be hard – our brains are wired to favor the new and exciting task over the tired one you've been working at. One of the purposes of the board is to protect you from that instinct. Resist any urge to put partially completed work back in the "To Do" column; you want to establish a smooth left-to-right flow.

You also will almost certainly over estimate the number of tasks you can accomplish in a day. There are actually two cognitive biases that conspire to cause this: the planning fallacy and the optimism bias. The former causes us to over-estimate our capacity to deliver work and the latter makes us under-estimate the difficulty of a particular piece of work.[21] Another purpose of the kanban board is to help you become better at estimating; both your capacity for work and the scope of individual tasks.

On the other hand, if you're like many people you'll enjoy the visual nature of the tool—especially as you watch your completed tasks stack up in the "Done!" column. The trade-off for mono-tasking is the little squirt of dopamine you'll get from getting things over the line (and off your plate).

If kanban-for-a-day works for you, try it again tomorrow (clean out your "Done!" column each night, but leave unfinished tasks on the board). As you prioritize your next-day's tasks, you'll have to decide whether they move above yesterday's unfinished (technically un-started) work in the "To-Do" column and arrange your stickies accordingly.

As I mentioned earlier, you may decide you need to add a few columns to the left of "To-Do" to help you prioritize work a little farther into the future. I recommend a "Tomorrow" column, and then possibly a "This Week" and maybe a "Later." Many folks also add a "Waiting" column between "Doing" and "Done!" for those tasks where you've done all you can, but someone else's effort is needed to get it over the line (or back to you to complete). Set a WIP limit for each of your columns so you don't put too much in flight.

This brief intro only scratches the surface of Productivity Kanban (sometimes known as Personal Kanban[22]), but even this little bit will help you start to manage competing demands on your time and attention. If you have team members, encourage them to try this method also; it can help get everyone aligned on group-level capacity and prioritization.

Kanban for routine processes

Although Kanban can be excellent for mapping complex processes, using it for your routine work will yield a solid return. Whereas Productivity Kanban is useful when managing different types of tasks and different sources of input, Workflow Kanban is best for managing multiple projects (matters or cases) through a common process.

Although the steps are a little more involved than with Productivity Kanban, they are still fairly straightforward:

1. You'll need a little more space on your wall or whiteboard. A 3x5 whiteboard is about as small as you can get away with, and 4x6 is about right for most teams.
2. Draw five lines to create six columns on the board.
3. Label them from left-to-right with something like the following: "Intake," "Research," "Drafting," "Review & Revise," "Execute," and "Finalize."[23] Tweak the labels however you want to best fit your team's terminology.
4. Grab a pack of sticky notes. Instead of writing tasks on them as above, you'll write the name of a matter you're working on (or another unique project identifier) on each card.
5. Put each card in the column of the board that best corresponds to the current phase of that project/matter. Items that need attention soon should go to the top of each column, with lower-priority matters lower down.
6. Grab a fresh sheet of paper (or, if you have room, you can do this directly on the whiteboard). For each column, write down a "Definition of Done" checklist that captures all of the things that need to be true or accounted-for before a matter leaves that phase. Keep it high-level; no more than 8-10 items for each column (and 3-4 is fine too). Tape that checklist on the board over the relevant column. This is a rough quality control tool as well as a backflow check valve to make sure matters flow from left-to-right and not the other way.

7. Meet frequently with your team in front of the board. Ideally hold a short daily stand-up meeting.[24] Each team member should answer three questions: "What did I do yesterday (to move matters forward)?" "What do I plan to do today (to move matters forward)?" and "What roadblocks (if any) are in your way?"[25]
8. Move cards through the board as appropriate. And repeat the standup meeting regularly[26] to help generate accountability among team members, instill a sense of ownership, and stay on top of any bottlenecks that arise.

Workflow Kanban provides excellent visibility and accountability for teams that embrace it. By seeing where individual matters stand in relation to the overall process, team members get a better sense of the purpose of individual tasks and of progress (or lack thereof) for individual matters. It also helps improve communication among team members by drawing their focus towards the work and workflow and away from the perceived shortcomings of any individual workers.

As with Productivity Kanban, this illustration is just a high-level way to get started with a Workflow Kanban approach. Even this simple structure, however, can be helpful for improving the flow of work through a workflow. There are many ways to build it out further, including adding queue stages (where work is waiting on availability of a resource), adding horizontal swim lanes to track different matter types, and fleshing out the cards themselves with rich information about the matter.

With both methods, it can be helpful to keep in mind the five rules of Kanban:

- Make the work, and the workflow, visible;
- Make policies explicit;
- Limit WIP;
- Measure and manage flow; and
- Improve, iteratively, with data.

Finally, Productivity Kanban and Workflow Kanban can work in conjunction with each other. Many teams will use a Workflow method to track the high-level phases of their work, but individual workers will then use Productivity Kanban to manage the individual tasks they take away from the daily standup.

Potential pitfalls

As with any new methodology or initiative, implementing Agile is not without risks. Change is hard in any setting, more so in a profession with a strong allegiance to precedent. As with any change efforts, it is important not to imbue Agile with too much power. I believe Agile is significantly better than traditional ways of managing legal work, but it is not perfect.

Nor is it magical. Unlike many whiz-bang technologies that promise overnight success, Agile is more conventional improvement advice: adjust your habits, put in the work, and learn from mistakes. What sets Agile apart is that embracing change is part of its DNA. Teams that use it to become learning organizations will better position themselves to adapt to evolving needs.

Some specific problems that may arise that could hamper your progress toward Agility include:

- Difficulty un-learning old habits. Agile helps teams deliver value more efficiently, but for legal professionals with traditional backgrounds (especially those who have worked in large firms), this can be hard to absorb. Efficiency is not the friend of the billable hour, and people who built their habits around hours targets often push back against more productive ways of working.
- Lack of executive support. While I have seen some examples of ground-up Agile transformations, I've seen just as many such efforts quashed by management that doesn't support – or doesn't understand – the goals of Agile teams. Agile transformations take time, and there is often a "messy middle" when teams are letting go of old ways of working but aren't yet comfortable with the new. Executive support and encouragement are essential to giving team members the psychological safety they need to power through the transition.
- Too much attention to dogma. At its core, Agile is more a philosophy than a strict methodology. Still, many people make their livings on teaching a specific shape of peg, round holes be damned. It is far more important to *be* agile than to *do* Agile, and a willingness to abandon tools that aren't working and experiment with new ones will go a long way toward the former.
- The busy trap.[27] Some teams have members who thrive on the notion of being "busy." Often their identities are inextricably intertwined with busy-ness. There is an important distinction between being

busy and being productive, and Agile favors the latter. It also favors visibility of work and transparency among team members, features that can rob "busy" people of their favorite shield. Unless leaders make special efforts to assure these people that they still have important roles even if they aren't running ragged, I have seen busy-loving individuals attempt to sabotage Agile efforts in order to preserve their favored identity.

Empowering technologies

I teach introductory Agile workshops several times a year, and with all my talk of whiteboards and sticky notes there is inevitably someone who says, "This is interesting and all, but surely there is some software tool that does all this for you, right?"

The short answer is yes, there are many such tools, but you're not ready for them when you're just getting started. Part of what makes Agile work is its visual nature, but there is lot to be said for the physical, tangible elements as well. Teams I've worked with come to relish the feeling of grabbing a kanban card and moving it through the various stages of their board until it gets to "Done." For knowledge workers who normally don't physically interact with their work, having that tangible stand-in can be exhilarating.

Besides, there are three strong advantages of a physical board. First, the learning curve for whiteboards and sticky notes is essentially zero. While you have to draw a few lines, nobody has to configure any software and nobody needs to be trained on how it works. This also makes prototyping and iteration easier. Don't like where a line is drawn or how a column is labeled? Erase it and re-do it; no programming necessary.

Second, unless you want to shell out thousands of dollars on a Jumbotron-sized display, few computer monitors can match the size and scale of a whiteboard. A kanban board is meant to be an information radiator, helping the team understand not only what work to prioritize, but how and why. Computer screens make it hard to fit everything in.

Physical boards also let you easily see the work at different levels of abstraction. Need to know exactly what is going on with the TPS report? Zoom in (by walking closer to the board) on that card to read its details. Need to get a feel for bottlenecks in your overall workflow? Take a few steps back to take in the big picture.

Finally, unlike windows on a computer screen or tabs in a web browser, it is hard to lose track of a wall. Physical boards have a presence, and a persistence, that helps the team stay on course.

Physical boards, of course, have some downsides too. Updates require physically going to where the board is. They can be harder to coordinate for remote team members. And, when you get to the point of your Agile journey when you're ready to start analyzing metrics, physical boards can't automate data collection like software tools can.

My rule of thumb is to start simple and add complexity only when you can articulate a clear advantage for doing so. Physical boards are dead-simple. At the very least, I recommend that teams use a physical board for several weeks, or until the structure of their board stabilizes. Doing so will make an eventual transition to a software-based board go much more smoothly.

If and when you decide to move to a software tool, here too I advise starting with simple tools. The best-known product is Trello, and I know many teams who use it to great success.[28] Beware that although it is possible to use Trello as a kanban board, it is not inherently an Agile tool. In other words, don't confuse using Trello with being Agile – you still need to learn the methodology.

If your business uses Microsoft Office 365, you already have access to Microsoft Planner, a Trello-like program that interacts well with other Microsoft software. Other popular tools include Asana and Monday.com, both of which let users switch between kanban view and other project-management interfaces.

If simple tools aren't quite meeting your needs, there are several mid-level programs that offer more complex configurations for your boards as well as more robust reporting. My two favorites in this area are LeanKit and Kanbanize. These require more up-front setup efforts, but they can be a good upgrade for teams who need one.

At the high-end, you may be able to leverage enterprise Agile software that your business is already using. Some popular tools include Jira, VersionOne, and Pivotal Tracker. These are very robust programs that will likely require a dedicated resource for configuration and maintenance.

Finally, I know of at least one software tool that is specifically targeted to in-house legal teams looking to adopt Agile methods: BigFork Technology's ALOE (short for Automated Legal Ops Environment). Interestingly, ALOE is built on top of the Jira engine, but with many of the software-specific elements stripped away and several legal-friendly tools added. Although I have not yet used it personally, I am closely following its development.

Conclusion

The Agile method's popularity has seen rapid growth in its relatively short history, initially among technology teams but increasingly throughout the enterprise. Agile's focus on quality, value, and productivity make it well-suited for the in-house legal team, and GCs are increasingly harnessing its benefits. While it isn't magic, Agile teams typically realize significant improvements to both productivity and morale vs their previous methods.

The best way to get started with Agile is to just get started: Do some research, get familiar with the tools and terminology, and then run an experiment yourself. It might not go exactly as you hope, but either way you'll gain valuable insight into what works and what doesn't. That learning is how you'll know you're on your way to a more Agile legal practice.

References

1. The Agile Manifesto, https://agilemanifesto.org
2. VersionOne, Inc, 11th Annual State of Agile Report (2017). https://www.versionone.com/about/press-releases/versionone-releases-11th-annual-state-of-agile-report/
3. Darrel K. Rigby, Jeff Sutherland, & Andy Nobel, Agile at Scale, *Harvard Business Review*, (May-June 2018). https://hbr.org/2018/05/agile-at-scale
4. Anthony Davis, How In-House Legal Departments Can Become Truly Innovative, *Lexpert* (February 2016). https://www.lexpert.ca/article/how-in-house-legal-departments-can-become-truly-innovative]
5. An emphasis here on intrinsic, as opposed to extrinsic, motivation. In other words, people who are driven by an interest in the work itself – because of the nature of the problems being solved or a desire to help the customers who will benefit from the solution, or both. Contrast with extrinsic motivators like efforts-based compensation. This distinction is the core of Daniel Pink's excellent book Drive: The Surprising Truth About What Motivates Us (Riverhead Books, 2009).
6. Physical safety is, of course, important, but Agile practitioners strongly emphasize psychological safety as well.
7. *See*, e.g. *If Russ Ackoff Had Given a Ted Talk*, https://youtu.be/OqEeIG8aPPk.
8. In knowledge work, unlike in manufacturing, there is relatively little physical waste. But process- or activity-oriented waste is rampant.
9. I use "customer" instead of "client" because, although the client is important and always an end-customer, it is not always the immediate customer for a particular process.
10. Kevin Kelly, The Inevitable; Understanding the 12 Technological Forces That Will Shape Our Future, 11 (Viking 2016).
11. Eric Reis, The Lean Startup: How Today's Entrepreneurs Use Continuous Innovation to Create Radically Successful Businesses, 9, (Crown Business Publishing 2011).

12. Named for W. Edwards Deming, Engineer and a forefather of the Toyota Production System, more commonly known in the west as Lean Manufacturing.
13. Leaving the retrospective for the end makes sense in a project management context when the main priority is usually to deliver the work, and too much process improvement work could create instabilities that might disrupt that goal.
14. Kanban is a Japanese work meaning "sign." Use of kanbans is common in Lean Manufacturing and related methods as a signal from one part of a process to another, triggering the latter to perform some task or deliver inventory. It is typically pronounced "kahn-bahn," though the more Americanized "can-ban" is common.
15. Scrum-Ban is commonly a Kanban-style workflow with regular planning and review meetings borrowed from Scrum.
16. Kahneman's research partner Amos Tversky contributed substantially to the field of behavioral economics for which Kahneman was awarded the Nobel Price, but Tversky passed away before the awards and Nobels are not awarded posthumously.
17. Daniel Kahneman, *Thinking Fast and Slow* (Farrar, Straus and Giroux 2013).
18. Many legal professionals with a law firm background understand the term WIP to mean "hours we've worked but haven't yet billed." While that is one source of work in progress, in the Agile context we define WIP to mean any work that has been started but not fully delivered.
19. Multitasking is now widely regarded as an inefficient way to work. As with juggling, each new task requires the worker to spend more time and attention tracking the balls in the air rather than working on the matter at hand. *See, e.g.*, Travis Bradberry, *Multitasking Damages Your Brain And Career, New Studies Suggest*, *Forbes*, (October 8, 2014) (https://www.forbes.com/sites/travisbradberry/2014/10/08/multitasking-damages-your-brain-and-career-new-studies-suggest/#7d1d777856ee)
20. Yes, many digital checklist tools allow for drag and drop reprioritization, which is better, but in my experience still doesn't do as good a job with context as kanban.
21. *Freakonomics* covered this in its radio / podcast episode 323, "Here's Why All Your Projects Are Always Late – and What to Do About It." http://freakonomics.com/podcast/project-management/.
22. *See, e.g.* Jim Benson & Tonianne DeMaria Barry, *Personal Kanban: Mapping Work | Navigating Life* (Modus Cooperandi Press 2011).
23. For litigation, the generic workflow stages are "Intake," "Pleadings," "Written Discovery," "Oral Discovery," "Dispositive Motions," "Pre-Trial," and "Trial." I recognize that not all litigation is quite so linear so that more complex board structures might be necessary, but I've worked with several litigation teams who use Kanban to great effect.
24. The use of daily standups is common in Scrum. My rule-of-thumb for a stand-up meeting length is that it should be no longer than 90 seconds for each team member.

25. If you are a team leader or manager, your highest and best use is to remove roadblocks for everyone else before moving on to your own tasks.
26. Practice has shown that short daily standups outperform weekly (or less-frequent) planning meetings because they ensure consistent progress and surface problems sooner (thereby allowing them to be addressed sooner). See, e.g. Jason Yip, *It's Not Just Standing Up: Patterns for Daily Standup Meetings*, MartinFowler.com (2016) (https://www.martinfowler.com/articles/itsNotJustStandingUp.html).
27. Called after Tim Kreider's popular 2012 opinion piece for the *New York Times*, https://opinionator.blogs.nytimes.com/2012/06/30/the-busy-trap/.
28. If you decide to go with Trello, be aware that its free tier has limited data security features. Most teams will need a paid plan to comply with legal ethics rules and company data security policies. Obviously, whatever software you use, you should be familiar and comfortable with its data, security, and/or encryption policies.

Chapter 7:
A case for working with your colleagues in the procurement department

By Dr Silvia Hodges Silverstein and Dr Lena Campagna, executive director and research and education director of the Buying Legal Council

Many large organizations have a procurement department dedicated to sourcing legal services. These departments leverage the unique experience of dedicated professionals trained in data analysis and sourcing technology to manage spending and increase efficiency in hiring outside counsel. Professional procurement and spend management is an area where most general counsel and their in-house lawyers have had minimal training in law school and only limited professional experience. Together, they can have significant impact on their organization's bottom line.

Organizations benefit from involving procurement in many ways, including:

- Actively managing external legal spend and identifying opportunities for innovative cost arrangements;
- Improving the efficiency and robustness of the process to identify the best vendors;
- Identifying and managing the best value legal services, ensuring that providers deliver value;
- Helping unbundle legal services and match them to the most appropriate providers;
- Measuring and demonstrating the value the legal function delivers to the organization; and
- Optimizing the business side of relationships with law firms and other legal services providers.

As you read this, allow us to demonstrate the urgency of legal procurement for your organization. Research from the international legal procurement trade organization Buying Legal Council highlights that involving legal procurement is instrumental in cutting costs and streamlining spending on outside counsel. According to the *2018 Buying Legal Council Legal Procurement Survey* (downloadable at www.buyinglegal.com/survey), organizations involving procurement professionals save an average of 15 percent on their legal spend. That number jumps to an astonishing 21 percent for organizations that devote more effort to the process. This is a considerable amount, and without doubt the key reason top management embraces legal and procurement's collaboration. Even ten years after the 2008 financial crisis, most organizations still look to cut costs where they can, and the numbers demonstrate legal procurement provides an effective way to do just that.

The benefits of legal procurement go well beyond just the bottom line. In the absence of legal procurement's involvement, some of its work would not be done at all or done by the legal department. The work legal procurement departments typically take on – including issuing, managing, and evaluating requests for proposal (RFP), fee analytics and negotiations, benchmarking, developing and enforcing billing guidelines – are arguably not the most efficient use of a general counsel's and their in-house counsel's time. Having this type of work accomplished by specialized professionals frees up in-house counsel to focus on what they were trained to do – the actual legal work.

What does it take? Achieving success in procurement

Legal procurement professionals are most successful when able to use a variety of procurement approaches, including working with a preferred provider list of outside law firms, implementing billing guidelines, sending RFPs, using alternative fee arrangements (AFAs) or project-based budgets, negotiating discounted hourly rates, conducting invoice audits, and working with alternative legal service providers. In the above mentioned *2018 Legal Procurement Survey*, that list contrasted sharply with the limited number of tactics employed by procurement professionals who self-identified in the Survey as being the "least successful". The survey revealed a likely explanation for this discrepancy: tenure. The longer a legal procurement professional has worked in legal services, the more likely she was to use the full range of procurement tools and activities in their support of the legal department.

Perhaps unsurprisingly, the more collaborative the relationship between a legal department and procurement, the more effective procurement professionals feel they can be. The relationship between procurement and legal is a key driver for success. The more that this looks like a partnership, the greater cost-savings for their employer — which, in turn, reflects favorably on the general counsel and their legal department. When legal and procurement work together, top management do not have to worry about runaway or unprofessionally managed legal costs.

With legal procurement's help, legal departments can move away from the traditional "passive" approach to managing legal spend to a more "active" or even "collaborative" approach: from maintaining policies and procedures that encourage self-regulation of legal spend management (but take little direct influence on benefits and savings), to active engagement with outside counsel, ensuring policies and procedures are followed and benefits and savings are realized. The "collaborative" management approach goes even further to include developing shared accountability between outside counsel and in-house lawyers to deliver innovative solutions.

How can procurement deliver tangible results in managing your legal spend?

Legal spend management initiatives can range from simple process or policy changes to more complex and comprehensive programs. In order to decide which legal spend management initiatives to worth pursuing, Peter Eilhauer and Matt Todd of Elevate recommend taking into consideration an organization's time horizon, culture, and expectations. In the *Legal Procurement Matrix*, they mapped legal spend management initiatives accordingly:

- **Time to Achieve Benefits** forms the x-axis of the matrix: strategies in the left quadrants typically realize benefits more quickly than strategies in the right quadrants;
- **Change Management Requirements** form the y-axis of the matrix: strategies in the bottom quadrants tend to be easier to deploy — either technically or politically — than strategies in the top quadrants;
- **Benefit Opportunities** are determined by the size of the bubbles in the matrix: larger bubbles show strategies that are more likely to deliver greater cost savings than strategies indicated by smaller bubbles.

Such a mapping exercise details the pros and cons of different cost-savings initiatives and strategically approaches legal spend management.

The matrix below shows an example of such a mapping exercise and includes several common legal spend management initiatives:

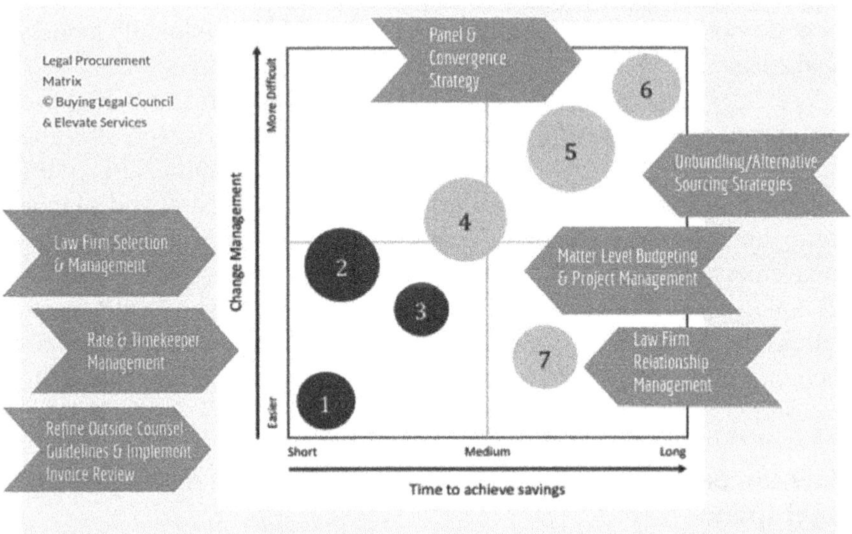

Figure 1: The Legal Procurement Matrix

Source: Buying Legal Council Legal Spend Management Primer: The Practical Guide to Strategic Legal Spend Management Initiatives (by Peter Eilhauer and Matt Todd, Elevate) Downloadable at www.buyinglegal.com/LSM

A legal department that requires fast cost control measures might select projects in the bottom-left quadrant, while an organization looking for larger and long-term benefits might consider projects in the top right quadrant. Please note that it is not necessary to implement initiatives chronologically (from one to seven).

Let us briefly discuss the various approaches:

1. Clients should develop **outside counsel guidelines** to provide legal services providers with their expectations regarding billing procedures. Outside counsel guidelines identify which tasks and expenses are compensable and outline the format for outside counsel's billing requirements. When developing outside counsel guidelines, clients need to be clear about their expectations and the consequences for failing to meet these expectations. If expectations are not met, clients run the risk to be challenged by their outside counsel. **Legal invoice review** is the process of applying outside counsel guidelines to law firm invoices and adjusting any non-compliant invoices. While

legal departments traditionally "review" invoices before payment, a strategic legal invoice review includes a two-step workflow where a centralized invoice review team conducts the initial review; the in-house lawyer then reviews the invoice. This ensures consistency in how reviews are conducted and reduces administration time for in-house lawyers. While in-house counsel may be concerned that adjusting bills negatively impacts the relationship with their firms, a professionally conducted invoice review that adheres to best practices, adjusts for clear guideline violations, and bears in mind the spirit of the invoice and the overall relationship will minimize disruption and encourage a healthy program.

2. **Law firm selection and management** means strategically assigning matters to law firms and legal services providers to ensure the right "fit" and quality. For example, high-volume, low complexity matters should not be assigned to the same law firms as highly complex matters and vice versa. Strategic law firm selection and management necessitate a formalized, controlled, and consistent approach across the legal department. They include matter scoping; selecting of firm(s) to approach; using competitive commercial processes such as requests for proposal or even (online) auctions; negotiation processes based on clearly defined proposal details and success criteria; recording the engagement, its scope, commercial aspects and underlying assumptions; as well as tracking the matter in a "living" document and updating it throughout the duration of the matter.

3. Most legal departments do not have a comprehensive method for verifying whether rates charged are within a reasonable range for the type of the work performed. Collecting, processing, and approving timekeepers and rates put significant operational strain on in-house counsel. As a consequence, in-house counsel often either "automatically" approve rates and new timekeepers (which increases costs and risk) or conduct one-off negotiations that may add as much cost as the problem they aim to solve. **Rate and timekeeper management** is intended to reduce lawyer's administrative time and to separate rate conversations from management of the overall relationship. Rate and timekeeper management includes the approval of annual rate increases as well as the intake and approval of new timekeepers added to new or existing matters. An efficient way to manage rates and timekeepers is to direct work to an invoice processing team with clearly defined roles and an objective approval

system. It centralizes rate requests, processes them according to a defined set of criteria, uses one's own data as well as industry benchmarking date, and manages the onboarding of new timekeepers or rates to ensure entries are compliant.

4. The purpose of **matter-level budgeting and project management** is to set clear cost expectations and a project plan for each matter. It necessitates collecting information and analyzing budgets to control previously unknown spend. It should be done at the outset of a matter, either as a competitive bid or as a single budget request. Project management in this context is intended to encourage visibility into spend on the matter, to predict spend increases or decreases, and to proactively manage any changes in the overall budget. Budgeting and project management can substantially impact overall legal spend. Applied properly, over time, legal budgets should become accurate. This may reduce traceable cost savings (calculating benefits based on write-offs), as well as result in a reduction of overall spend and cost per matter phase and task. More than any other strategy, budgeting and project management requires the right tools and technologies in place to measure and monitor budgets, variances, and cost savings.

5. **Unbundling and alternative sourcing** is intended to optimize the allocation of legal resources. Alternate sourcing aims to reduce cost and turnaround times for legal services by utilizing third-party legal resources (so-called alternative or ancillary legal services providers) instead of in-house resources or traditional outside counsel. Unbundling is the exercise of identifying distinct legal tasks that can be separated and completed individually. Tasks can be assessed for complexity, volume, and priority. Once discrete tasks are identified and considered, a process flow can be tailored to coordinate work between in-house counsel and third party resources.

6. **Panel convergence** is the process of creating or refining panels of preferred provider firms and setting appropriate rates via a comprehensive request for proposal. Legal departments can have hundreds of outside counsel firms supporting them on a wide variety of work. The work can vary by matter type, risk and complexity, jurisdiction, etc. While most firms will default to hourly rates, there are cases where law firms offer alternative fee arrangements such as fixed and flat fees, fee caps and collars, in addition to discounts.

7. **Law firm relationship management** is the concept of formalizing relationships and objectives between the law firm and the legal department. Business reviews set expectations and facilitate developing a mutually beneficial relationship. While the content of a business review depends on the maturity of the relationship with the firm, a full review includes both a quantitative review to analyze spend trends and cost variances as well as a qualitative review, including measuring performance against company-defined goals or service levels. In addition, a collaborative review includes shared goals, aimed to identify or track progress on common initiatives. It is important that the review focuses on driving results. To be scalable, the organization should develop a template to uniformly collect business review metrics.

Legal procurement: where do we go from here?

The main takeaway is that the general counsel has a significant role to play in legal services procurement. Procurement professionals can professionally support the general counsel and her team in the legal department in the whole range of legal spend management initiatives. When in-house counsel and legal procurement professionals collaborate, they contribute directly to their employer's success.

For general counsel, the best course of action is clear: give procurement professionals a chance to prove themselves. Once that hurdle is cleared, it is imperative that the general counsel trusts these professionals to be an asset going forward. It may take time and patience to develop a tolerance for new protocol and strategies, but the rewards – both monetary and otherwise – will be well worth it.

In his foreword to the *Legal Procurement Handbook* (2015), DuPont's former general counsel Tom Sager states: "So like it or not, we need to apply every conceivable strategy, methodology, and tool available to us to deliver value to our common client. And meet budget! It is like making a mortgage payment. You simply cannot afford to miss it." Procurement can help. Contact your chief procurement officer today if you do not already work with their department. Be a part of this exciting process and watch the transformation of effectiveness and efficiency.

Chapter 8: The valued legal department and legal ops – a strategy for success

By Steven A Lauer, principal of Lauer & Associates, and Ken Vermilion, principal of The Vermilion Group Strategic Legal Management LLC

A couple of decades ago, law departments began to recognize that the challenge of managing those departments' resources – both internal and external – represented a growing and ever more challenging aspect of the general counsel's responsibilities. The growth of those responsibilities did nothing to reduce any of the substantive aspects of their jobs, which also became increasingly complex. Moreover, those new responsibilities related to areas and types of expertise with which lawyers had been unfamiliar by training. Accordingly, law departments began to invest in individuals to whom they assigned that management responsibility, often accompanied by a title like "vice president – operations" or something similar. Such an individual thereby could free up the time that the chief legal officer or general counsel (for simplicity, let's use the term "GC" to include individuals with either title) otherwise would have had to devote to those tasks.

Since the operational role in a corporate law department first appeared, it has become an increasingly pivotal one within organizational structures and even in the legal profession generally, as the value that it adds to the department has become more clearly recognized. Law departments' operations executives no longer merely take over the more ministerial aspects of the general counsel's responsibilities. Rather, the individuals charged with improving the operations of corporate law departments have specialized to an increasing degree in managing the inchoate service for which those departments are responsible. This, of course, has allowed the GC to fulfill more easily the role of strategic counselor to the organization by allowing him or her to offload those responsibilities, which have significant non-legal components and therefore require less substantive knowledge, that otherwise consume so much time and effort. That increased specialization, in turn, has paralleled the increasing assertiveness of the in-house bar in respect of how lawyers service corporate clients.

With the emergence and continued development of that role, more GCs face the issues of (i) whether to add such a position in their departments and (ii) if so – or if their departments already employ individuals in such a role – how best to utilize that resource. What value can an operations executive add to the department? How would such a resource assist the GC? How can the GC maximize the benefit of such a position for the organization?

That challenge directly relates to the ultimate purpose of the search, on the part of corporate law departments, for greater value in the legal service that they create, secure and manage for their companies. With the unceasing pressure to deliver superior service for a lower (or, at least, no higher) cost than previously, in-house lawyers must determine how to calibrate the demand for the service and the service delivered more accurately. Buying an "A" defense in a "C" case will not satisfy corporate executives who challenge all other parts of the business enterprise to be as lean and effective as possible (if ever it truly did satisfy them).

Phase I: the emergence of the law department operations executive and that individual's early focus

Legal department operations staff began to bubble up more frequently beginning with the financial and economic meltdown that began in 2008. Corporations were putting extreme pressure on all divisions and departments to cut costs and to do much more with fewer resources. For what was often the first time, chief executive officers (CEOs) and chief financial officers (CFOs) were looking at legal departments with a lens focused on reducing costs. This lens, however, was cloudy at best, because CEOs and CFOs, as well as the GC's peers, really didn't understand how the legal departments functioned. They did understand, however, that a pretty big number appeared on the profit-and-loss statement next to the entry for "legal department expenses." They reasoned that if the human resources department or finance and maintenance can be expected to reduce spend by 20 percent, the law department should be equally capable of reducing its spend.

GCs that were considered early adopters of the "operations executives model" identified at least three critical areas that needed addressing if their legal departments were to improve their performance. These areas were to better understand budgets and costs, to ensure that department processes and procedures were as efficient as possible, and to see that all staff leveraged technology effectively. After a year or two, legal departments of those forward-thinking GCs were demonstrating improved performance.

This new breed of legal department management executives had also figured out how to communicate this improved state of performance in terms that the CFO and CEO could understand, which was no small task. Other successes led to better skills matching and selection of outside counsel, successful leveraging of in-house skills sets, better utilization of the ever-expanding industry of alternative legal service providers (ALSPs), and the eventual emergence of AFAs where the first "A" stands for Appropriate, not Alternative.

With meaningful operational successes under the GC's belt on account of the presence of operations executives, it was time to shift the latters' focus to more strategic issues. We began to see the operations executives become involved in organizational matters, more sophisticated financial management, the expanded use of technology, and critical working relationships and partnerships across the corporation.

At the request of the GC, an operations executive might drive the analysis and conversation regarding whether a centralized legal organization served the corporation best or if a decentralized structure was better, or whether a mix of centralized and decentralized operations would maximize the department's impact. For example, centralize litigation, intellectual property, mergers and acquisitions and real estate, while embedding lawyers with their internal clients for labor and employment, regulatory matters, contracts and marketing. Operations executives were charged to collaborate with human resources professionals to upgrade recruiting and onboarding processes. Operations executives also managed projects, often in conjunction with specialized outside consultants, to develop competitive compensation plans and sorely missing leadership development programs for the legal staff. Leadership topics for lawyers included an emphasis on developing business acumen and skills, business communications skills, project management skills, and risk avoidance strategies, all intended to enable in-house lawyers better to serve as valuable and valued business partners for those clients – enablers rather than blockers. Practice section managers were schooled on the advantages and importance of diversity and inclusion.

With fundamental reporting of legal department costs and analysis of electronic billing data and the other drivers of legal department costs in place, the bar of legal department financial management needed to rise. The inside lawyers needed a clearer line of sight into their responsibilities to manage costs and enforce department outside counsel guidelines, since they were being asked to better manage large portfolios of diverse legal matters more often than simply taking ownership of a few discrete matters. Budget processes needed to be more credible, with added rigorous tracking and communication of the need for midcourse corrections (it is always a challenge to develop a twelve-month fiscal budget when a large portion of legal department work either transcends a twelve-month period or when new and significantly problematic matters unexpectedly arise during that period.)

Operations executives began to focus on management of outside counsel costs and to push the envelope on the use of the traditional hourly rate billing model as the sole basis for valuing work. At their instigation, the law departments often demanded that their external lawyers use ALSPs where the risk profile, knowledge management issues and costs offered by ALSPs aligned with department objectives and guidelines. Work was steered from law firms to more appropriate service providers at significantly reduced costs. Outside counsel were directed to partner and collaborate with these providers or risk losing other precious work.

Operations executives were also called upon to facilitate long-range strategic planning initiatives. Ensuring efficient legal processes requires the deployment of technology and a framework to ensure the utilization of technology by legal department staff, especially lawyers. Resources must be strategically invested in technology, which often had to be customized to produce quantifiable returns, to ensure the execution of uniform processes and to eliminate redundancies and harvest institutional knowledge. Legal department systems needed to integrate within the department's technology architecture where the sharing of data improved department management. Those systems often must talk with other corporate systems, e.g. accounts payable, company unit databases, and human resources. As the use of technology matured, legal departments began to contemplate the development of in-department technology support staff to help with the training, use and maintenance of specialized legal department systems.

Another focus for legal department operations was acquisition and integration of new hardware. Lawyers clamored for handheld units that behaved exactly like their desktops to enable them to work anytime and anywhere if need be. Laptops needed to securely connect to legal department servers from outside the corporation's firewall, and data in motion needed to be encrypted. These abilities improved departmental flexibility and significantly contributed to important "work/life balance" initiatives.

Operations executives' scope of responsibilities often expanded to include processes to improve outside counsel management, management of ALSPs, communication with CFOs, CEOs, public relations, audit committees, and boards of directors, to name a few. Though operations executives first cut their teeth on electronic bill analysis and other cost management analysis, their main concerns morphed to serving as drivers of change and innovation within the departments. Yes, legal department operations executives were strategic legal department management partners.

Phase II: analyzing existing data regarding the organization's use of legal service

As operations executives in law departments took charge of the operational aspects of those units, they surveyed the data available to their companies' in-house lawyers and the tools available to them in managing the departments' responsibilities. In many cases, the answers were less than satisfactory. While the profession had moved toward task-based billing and electronic transmission of law firms' invoices, thereby accelerating the processing of those invoices and eliminating some steps in that processing, the use and understanding of the data thereby generated remained immature. Accordingly, many of those professionals devoted their attention to analyzing and understanding the historical use of external resources by the departments.

Like it or not, for law departments (and, therefore, for the GC), managing costs does not suffice. Without an ability to demonstrate success in that regard and to illustrate how the law department creates value for the company, the GCs will find themselves continually on the hot seat. Unless they have educated their supervisors and executive peers regarding how the legal function works in that regard, cost reduction is the only activity that their peers, CFOs and many CEOs will be interested in and understand. Many GCs have faced this challenge: "Do you need all those lawyers? Especially when outside legal fees are so large and I can't get my contract reviewed in less than a month!" For that reason alone, creating or augmenting the department's capabilities to demonstrate that in terms that the CEO, CFO and others understand constitutes another significant responsibility. That part of the GC's responsibilities is one for which a qualified operations executive is well-suited.

In most legal departments, the portfolio of work can be broken down into two broad categories. One category could be called steady state work, which is pretty predictable. Data can be used to forecast employment claims work. Predictors could be the number of employees on payroll by state and/or by particular job these employees are assigned. Tort claims may be related to the amount of square footage the corporation manages and its business model and the jurisdictions in which it is licensed to conduct business. Forecasting legal costs related to constructing a new warehouse, call center or regional office should be predictable and steady based on growth plans of the corporation.

The other category would be anomaly matters. These anomaly matters can be few but represent a significant portion of outside legal services spend. You, as the reader, are in a position to identify those matters for your own organization better than the writer. That said, legal spend on outside legal services should be broken down into steady state legal work and anomaly costs.

Demonstrating cost containment and reporting comparative year over year data that demonstrates successful cost control is important. Raw costs, cost per tort matter, costs per contract, discovery costs as a percentage of total costs for similar matters, settlements related to costs to get to settlement, etc. are all possible analytics that could demonstrate cost containment, reduction and corresponding value of services.

There are a few rules that need to be followed when extracting the most value from legal department analytics. First, lawyers need to understand the fundamentals of the analytics applied to their productivity and to a large degree accept that the analytics are a reasonable yard stick to be integrated into their annual performance review, assuming an annual performance reviews program exists. Second, data can be hard financial comparisons and softer feedback from internal clients. Data used for performance evaluations must be significant enough in size to be meaningful and collected in a balanced and fair manner. Third, GCs need to demonstrate consequences for lack luster performance and rewards for stellar performance.

Phase III: data and value-related qualities underlie a more strategic understanding of "value"

The increasing maturity of the operational role has led to a recognition that those who fill that role should become more instrumental in utilizing that information in the law departments' possession to develop a more strategic vision. This, of course, flows from developments in law departments generally. The old paradigm of managing the work as it arises has proven inadequate in today's world of constant demands for greater efficiency and effectiveness and the ever-greater need for lower cost. Meeting those demands and the accompanying expectations requires a much more strategic approach to that management responsibility. We are on the cusp of much more intimate and complete knowledge and understanding of the use and application of internal and external resources to serve the departments' companies in a more holistic and effective fashion.

One of the core issues pertinent to that effort relates to understanding whether and how the legal service in question adds "value" to the company's business operations. Though the Association of Corporate Counsel initiated a "conversation" within the legal profession on that topic, after more than a decade in that endeavor, the profession as a whole has reached no consensus on how to define "value" for lawyers or how to apply to what lawyers do for their corporate clients any definition that might emerge from that discussion.

Why should the GC concern themselves or the department with defining "value"? Why should law departments' operations executives devote resources to what might appear to be a quixotic endeavor? The short answer is that the definition, if properly developed, will enable the department to develop the optimal means of delivering the legal service needed for its company to achieve its business objectives in the most efficient, direct and least costly way. The GC will, in turn, find their job easier if the department's service to the organization revolves around an agreed-upon conception of how the legal service can best serve the company and enable that organization to achieve more effectively and efficiently its business objectives.

The definition will prove its usefulness in a myriad of ways. For example, incorporating that definition in the law department's strategic planning process will ensure that the various parties to that process and those impacted by it (e.g. corporate executives, law department leaders, outside counsel) have access to a singular, agreed-upon vision of the organization's anticipated need for legal service and the means by which its in-house lawyers plan to secure and manage that service. In another context, the decisions regarding whether specific assignments should be performed internally or externally, and in the latter case by which parties among the external providers available to the law department, can be made in a more deliberative, specific and defensible fashion.

In light of the experience with ACC's Value Challenge and the lack of a singular product of that exercise, can we identify another means of achieving a useable method by which to measure how well legal service satisfies clients' needs? Yes, if we train our vision on the underlying traits of legal service that increase or decrease its utility to the ultimate users, rather than focus on the broader definition. Those underlying traits, which we can call value-related qualities or "VRQs," will constitute much more useful tools with which to approach clients' needs.

How might that work? Consider that the same legal service or the same service provider might deliver vastly different value in distinct contexts. For example, a law firm that has developed a deserved reputation for successfully representing corporate clients in bet-the-company litigation, in which its value is unsurpassed, likely would be a poor choice for a slip-and-fall case. Its value in the latter case might even be negative if its approach to that simple (in terms of legal issues) matter yields a fee for the representation that exceeds the potential liability faced by the client in that matter.

Examples of VRQs include these: expertise, cost control, low cost, consistency, predictability, responsiveness, and speed of resolution. Note that VRQs may be characteristics of the service provider (e.g. the law firm or the alternative service provider), the specific need for legal service, the client, or even the individual(s) who might provide the service. A VRQ might reflect a positive or negative value in the particular situation in that the characteristic of the provider might add to or detract from how much the business client benefits from the service for the matter involved.

VRQs offer a great benefit to law departments (and to external counsel). Due to their discrete nature and their relationship to quantifiable aspects of the service or the provider or the situation, they lend themselves to measurement more readily than the vague term "value." Thus, VRQs can be taken into account in various methods of capturing data about law department operations, which has served as a prime focus on law department operations in the past. On account of the constant pressure to deliver – and to demonstrate the delivery of – legal service that enables the company to achieve its business objectives as effectively and as efficiently as possible, such measurability should serve as a primary advantage of this approach.

In that way, the VRQ approach dovetails nicely with the operations executives' previous focus on and analysis of data on law department performance. By extending that analysis to VRQs and their utility and application, the operations executives – and the law departments for which they work and the GCs to whom they report – will be better positioned to steer efforts toward those providers and approaches that more closely align with the departments' highest-value delivery and management of legal service.

When a law department has established its value profile using VRQs, it can turn its attention to counseling its external service providers in its value-related expectations and needs. Using measurable VRQs, it will be well-positioned to provide specific, actionable feedback to its outside law firms and other service providers when, and the extent to which, their service fails to meet those expectations or needs. VRQs can, therefore, empower in-house lawyers to manage their external collaborators in a much more useful way.

Phase IV: the operations executive leads the effort to define the "value" of the company's legal service

Corporate legal departments need to align law-related resources to ensure the biggest bang for the buck. They need to follow the money! This means that the departments' operations executives must be similarly focused.

Aligning resources needs to start with a plan. Best practice is to formally develop a strategic plan. Corporations used to step back from the activities of the day and prepare five-year strategic plans, but for a corporate law department five years almost equates with an eternity. The business world changes so much and so fast that we're seeing five-year planning exercises shrink to three-year exercises (it's critical, of course, that the law department's three-year strategic plan integrate with the company's strategic goals.)

Where does the GC want the legal department to be in three years? Elements of this plan may include, but are not limited to, these: What does the scope of in-house attorney work look like? Sketch out what kinds of work you expect that the attorneys will do, what additional responsibilities will be added, and what kinds of work might be eliminated. Cascading from that analysis is the impact on support staff, inventories of skill sets needed, and forecasting people costs and office space requirements;

- How does the use of outside counsel and third-party legal services providers supplement the nature of the envisioned legal work? Do trends in the legal services industry impact the allocation of work between in-house and external resources? Balancing proposed workloads is important;
- The articulation of a strategy for the continued deployment of law-specific technology and, if there are economies of scale and added efficiencies, where law department processes should leverage existing and planned corporate software and hardware technology platforms. What law department systems need to be retired, upgraded or procured? Does it generate a positive return on investment to develop client self-service, e.g. assemblage of high volume, relatively standard and low-risk contracts? Some

bleeding-edge operations executives are exploring the use of artificial intelligence as a productivity tool for data mining, analysis and predictive applications;

- Will the GC and corporate legal department expand their scope of responsibilities and accountabilities? Does the GC anticipate any change in his or her reporting relationship? Anticipating these possibilities, or even making a case for change, can significantly impact the need for resources; and
- The creation of a framework of key performance indicators (KPIs) and VRQs the department wants to improve.

The understanding that you have of the company's processes should enable you to add to these elements. It's also important to remember that the path to achieving goals related to strategic objectives is never a straight line. Changes in the business or economy, some other macro influence, or perhaps a surprise anomaly in legal work may necessitate mid-course corrections.

The strategic plan should drive the development of annual plans, which should contemplate areas of focus and necessary funding for those efforts, both expenses and capital investment. In establishing requisite funding requirements, the operations executive will begin to align or allocate resources with activities (tactics) that ultimately achieve various destination points mapped toward the achievement of the overall strategic plan.

In some corporate circles, it is believed that if your department isn't working on achieving key corporate objectives, you're working on the wrong things! A crisp understanding of the value proposition, as expressed in VRQs, that the law department develops allows the GC to drive the department toward a greater return on internal and external resources invested. The achievement of desired financial results and VRQs sets the stage for the allocation of resources that maximize value creation.

A significant element of a corporate legal department's ability to create value is the deployment of outside counsel and ALSPs. Let's address the selection of outside counsel first. Establishing the value that a law firm delivers to a client is not exclusively about the cash that changes hands as the result of the billing process. Although the cost of services may be the most quantifiable and visible expression of "value" for the client, progressive operations executives understand that measureable VRQs better serve to identify value-generating opportunities. E-billing and matter management systems provide a rich database that should be used in conjunction with a suite of performance metrics. The rigorous application of a multivariate selection tool may yield surprising results. Have faith in the model.

A similar framework of KPI and VRQs can be developed to support the selection of ALSPs. For this approach to work, the operations executive must have the full support of the GC.

Maximizing productivity yields on internal resources may be more art than science and include any combination of process reengineering, project management, performance evaluations, and change management. Generally speaking, the largest controllable expense on a law department's financial statement is employee compensation, especially that for the in-house attorneys. Ensuring peak performance from the attorney staff is essential to generating value for the corporation. To get that peak performance, the department must make investments in support of their work, such as investments in technology, appropriate support staff, and legal process tools that enable those attorneys to complete their jobs effectively and efficiently.

What's the best way to measure the return on the corporate legal department's investment in attorneys? The implementation of a *meaningful and behavior changing* process for evaluating attorney job performance is key. Performance expectations need to be clearly communicated and be supported with the metrics that will be used to evaluate performance. Performance evaluations need "teeth" and must be accompanied with consequences, good and bad. Only if they revolve around objective, measurable performance qualities (i.e. VRQs), however, will they serve the purpose well.

Process reengineering may be perceived as a daunting task, but it need not be. For example, our experience suggests that asking the people who perform processes to capture in writing the various steps they take is a good starting point. Next, have the people performing the tasks explain "why" things are done the way they are and explain the value that each step provides for the process. Generally, people doing the work will be the greatest resource contributing to reengineering a process. Quantifying benefits for changing to a new or revised process is the easy part. All this can and should be done utilizing VRQs.

Operations executives possess considerable strategic strengths – utilize them

The role of operations executive within a corporate law department offers considerable possibility for that department and its leader (the

GC). Particularly in respect of understanding how the department delivers value to the organization and assists that organization to achieve its business objectives (the ultimate *raison d'être* of the law department), that executive is well-prepared to move the department forward. By properly harnessing the strengths that an operations executive brings to the table, a GC will find herself or himself far better able to advocate for the law department's place at the table in corporate decision making and to strengthen the department's contributions in that regard. That, in turn, solidifies the GC's position within the enterprise.

Chapter 9:
Law department organizational design in an era of rapid change

By Jeffrey N Neuman, senior vice president, general counsel and corporate secretary of Tronox Limited

Introduction: doing two seemingly contradictory things at the same time

The goal of any organizational design initiative is to create structured roles and responsibilities that maximize the use of human talent, drive the right employee behaviors, and enable the corporation to achieve its strategic objectives. Designing a law department organization, whether to serve a publicly listed or private corporation, is no exception.

What sets law department organizational design principles apart is the law department's quasi-schizophrenic twin missions. First and foremost, the law department must be a trusted business partner, fully engaged with helping its clients achieve both their short- and long-term strategic goals. Simultaneously, the law department must protect the corporation's brand and reputation and ensure that the corporation's employees conduct themselves in accordance with the code of conduct and highest ethical standards. Successfully doing two seemingly contradictory things at the same time is common to many corporate functions. For example, human resource departments must simultaneously lower the corporation's labor expense and maintain high employee morale and an engaged workforce. Supply chain organizations must simultaneously reduce the amount of on-hand inventory and ensure on-time delivery. Law departments are no exception.

To resolve the seeming contradiction of being simultaneously a business partner and "cop-on-the-beat," law department organizational designs must emphasize client intimacy, facilitate each member's encyclopedic knowledge of the corporation's products, services, technologies and supply chain, and establish accountability for delivering results. Every first year law student learns that a winning legal argument is comprised of two components: the law and the facts. It is the in-house lawyer's job to be the master of the facts. Meaning that, regardless of whether a generalist or specialist, in-house legal roles must be designed to bring lawyers and paralegals into intimate and frequent contact with their clients and provide ample opportunities for lawyers to learn about the corporation's business. A trusted in-house lawyer, who has developed street credibility with his or her client, is in a much better position to protect the corporation's brand equity and uphold the code of conduct than an in-house lawyer who is removed and detached from the day-to-day tussle that characterizes most executive's professional lives.

The starting point: molding the law department's structure to the corporation

Because client intimacy is the bedrock of successful law department organizational design, the law department's organizational design must be tailored to the corporation's business model and its overall corporate organizational design. Is the corporation devoted to rapid revenue growth based on constant technological innovation and new product launch? Or is the corporation a "widow and orphan" stock where dependable delivery of quarterly EPS targets is paramount? Does the corporation operate in a highly regulated area like pharmaceuticals or aerospace, or is the corporation churning out undifferentiated widgets where the "secret sauce" is understanding the sales channel, effective marketing and maintaining cost discipline in the supply chain?

Regardless of the underlying industry or business model, most corporate organizations are built upon a "leadership team" structure. For each business division, segment or product unit, there is inevitably someone with responsibility for the income statement who has "P&L" responsibility. Around the "P&L leader" will be arrayed a variety of functions like sales, marketing and finance. In the case of a support organization like human resources, finance and treasury or research and development, there will nearly always be a functional leader, often with the title senior vice president, responsible for the support function. The law department should be organized based on the leadership team structure of the broader corporation so that each "P&L owner" or senior vice president has his or her assigned lawyer.

Client intimacy and getting a seat at the table

It is essential that the business unit lawyer or functional lawyer have an unquestioned seat at the leadership team table. The lawyer assigned to support the legal needs of the business unit or functional support must understand that being present at, and actively engaged in, all leadership team meetings is as important to professional success as contract drafting, advising on compliance matters, or preparing the annual proxy statement. The lawyer's goals and objectives must be tethered to, and aligned with, the goals and objectives of the relevant P&L leader or senior vice president. Each lawyer needs to understand that among the most important criteria for their career success or failure, including the annual compensation decision, will be direct feedback solicited from the P&L owner or senior vice president, as the case may be. When the leadership team travels, the lawyer travels, too.

Roles and responsibilities need to be designed with enough flexibility and space to accommodate full participation in leadership team activities, even if that involves such "non-legal" activities as plant tours, product demonstrations and customer visits. In small- and mid-sized companies, there will inevitably be overlap – the same lawyer who supports finance and treasury may also be required to support human resources, or the same lawyer who supports the P&L owner also supports the senior vice president for the supply chain. Regardless of the corporation's size, lawyers need to be encouraged to develop as much business acumen as legal knowledge, and to deploy both in providing top-notch client service to their clients.

But what about the "law" part of being an in-house lawyer? The design of a successful law department needs to be judicious in how it deploys specialist lawyers. Clearly, a technology company whose success is predicated on protecting its intellectual property needs strong intellectual property lawyers with relevant experience in prosecuting and defending patents in the appropriate field of use. Likewise, a bank or securities company needs lawyers with relevant financial institutional compliance experience to navigate the minutia of broker-dealer or "know your customer" regulations. The list of potential specialties required to best support the legal needs of a corporation is endless. Nonetheless, regardless of the degree of specialization, each in-house legal role needs to be designed to facilitate opportunities for the development and deployment of business acumen. Clients are much more likely to listen to, and follow the advice of, a lawyer who understands the business context and whose goals and objectives are firmly aligned to those of the relevant business unit or corporate function.

Minding cost: designing an organizational structure with champagne tastes but a Budweiser budget

The savvy law department organizational designer must of course always be conscious of cost. Designing a first-rate, in-house law department on a limitless budget is easy. Understandably, most corporations demand the same degree of cost accountability from their law department as they do for any other "functional" group whether finance, HR, procurement or communications. As a general rule of thumb, aggregate direct employee costs should represent approximately 0.20 percent of the corporation's total revenues. For a heavily regulated pharmaceutical company or financial institution, cost as a percentage of revenues will inevitably be higher as maintaining the "license to do business" is paramount and the regulatory burden is heavy. For a light manufacturer cranking out widgets, cost as a percentage of revenues will inevitably be lower.

Hence, all law departments regardless of size need one individual responsible for the budget. For a mid- or small-sized company, this will likely be a part-time job. Regardless, someone needs to have accountability for projecting costs – both employee-related costs and outside counsel – and delivering legal services to budget or at, the very least, providing analysis for variances. Publicly traded corporations are held to account by Wall Street for missing earnings by even $0.01 per share. Law departments must fight the mentality of entitlement. Too often, in-house lawyers believe that legal services are somehow "different" and should be exempt from the same strict cost and budget standards as research and development, procurement, human resources, or other corporate functions. A law department whose organizational design embraces cost discipline will invariably have more credibility with the corporation's leadership during occasions when difficult ethical or code of conduct decisions must be made.

For large law departments with substantial budgets – particularly for outside counsel spend – cost control and accurate cost projections can be a significant job, requiring an individual who is both numerate and has a solid of understanding of how legal services are delivered to the corporation and a willingness to think "outside the box". The role of "cost czar" is not typically thought of as "lawyer's work." But if the right individual is chosen, they can have an outsized impact on law department and even the entire company. In a large organization, the ability for the individual holding this role to partner with the colleagues in the business planning and analysis team and controllers group is critical.

Technology and innovation: part and parcel of law department organization design

Imagining new and innovative ways to deliver legal services, often involving deployment of emerging software technology, is an important part of cost control; the "cost czar" should therefore be part of all innovation initiatives. Ideally, every law department organizational design should have someone serving as "cost czar" and someone serving as chief innovation officer. Both roles can have an outsized impact on both law department effectiveness and the entire corporation.

Like so many key law department roles, organizational design is secondary to picking the right person. The law department's chief innovation officer should be an individual who truly believes that innovation and lawyering are not oxymorons, a real change agent. Unlike the world's oldest profession, technology offers a real opportunity for the legal profession to evolve. For law department organizational design, like with cost control, technological innovation happens only when an individual is accountable. Even if a part-time job, someone in every law department needs to have the moniker of "chief innovation officer". Like with cost control, the successful law department chief innovation officer will have the ability to re-imagine how legal services are delivered. From simple innovations like mandating electronic signatures to the development of software-based workflow tools for routine agreements and other common legal processes, the possibilities are endless and ever-increasing as the underlying software technology improves and evolves. Technology presents the opportunity to not only lower cost to serve, but also to improve quality and uniformity as well as to make the client experience superior. Best of all, technology presents the opportunity to gather data on what hereto seemed like a professional activity that couldn't be measured. How long does it take to prepare and complete a standard agreement? What are the most frequently amended provisions in our standard contracts? Utilizing software-based workflow tools for contracting versus the time-honored but inefficient bespoke drafting method is just one example of how the law department's chief innovation officer can make a big difference.

New frontiers: the role of the chief compliance officer and managing cyber risk

The creation of new roles like "cost czar" and "chief innovation officer" are not the only way that designing law department organizations have changed. Two other substantive areas have emerged where innovative organizational design is required: compliance and cybersecurity.

That compliance has emerged as one of the critical functions performed by most law departments is news to no one. The increasing importance to investors of "ESG" or environment, sustainability and governance attributes means that ethical lapses or compliance issues which once-upon-a-time were tolerated as the price of doing business are today seen as an ominous sign of a corrupt corporate culture, reason to dump the stock and, in the worst case scenarios, cause to launch an activist attack. A parallel trend that should also cause every law department to re-think the design of the compliance role is the greater importance that enforcement authorities place on a corporation's ability to tangibly demonstrate through hard data the presence of a meaningful compliance effort. The 2017 publication of the "Evaluation of Corporate Compliance Programs" by the Fraud Section of the US Department of Justice is but one example of the increasing expectations for the compliance function and how high the stakes have become. The ability of a top-notch compliance program now can mean the difference between prosecution and non-prosecution.

So what does this mean for organizational design? First and foremost, it means that the chief compliance officer needs to at least report to the general counsel and be a key member of their team, often with "dotted line" reporting to the chair of the audit committee or its equivalent. Second, the chief compliance officer needs to be connected to, and aligned with, the individual responsible for internal audit. This is important both to keep the initiatives and programs of the compliance function appropriately focused on the "right" risks and, depending on the risk area, to implement effective internal audit programs to ferret out little problems before they become big ones. Auditing of "travel and expense" and petty cash, particularly in high growth regions where corruption is prevalent, is but one example. Finally, the chief compliance officer needs to be plugged into the chief information officer and the IT organization. Whether developing a new "app" for approving gifts and entertainment expenses for state-owned enterprises in China, deploying training material across the enterprise via the corporation's "learning management system" or tracking employee allegations and complaints on the pan-corporate hotline tracking system, IT is more and more central to effective compliance.

Although usually core to the IT or security department's mandate, the relative criticality of cybersecurity to the corporation's risk profile should be considered as part of any law department organizational design. The degree of involvement by the law department in cybersecurity can vary widely: the needs of a healthcare company possessing its insureds' most sensitive personal data will be very different compared to a mining or manufacturing company with little "crown jewel" information and few employees. Depending on a corporation's cyber-risk profile, a law department role may be needed with responsibility for partnering with the IT or security department to participate in the corporation's cybersecurity defense initiatives and develop policies and procedures for handling the inevitable security breach. The role needs to be twofold: prophylactic, ensuring compliance with applicable cybersecurity standards and emerging regulations, such as the European Union's General Data Privacy Regulation or GDPR as well as reactive, triaging cyber incidences, assisting the technically-oriented cyber professionals think through liability issues, ensuring that the scope and severity of a cyber breach is communicated crisply and clearly to the myriad of stakeholders.

There is no one-size-fits-all law department organizational design. Each corporation needs to tailor the law department organizational design to both the corporation's own organizational structure and strategy. The only non-negotiable element for a law department organizational design is that roles and responsibilities must be created to enable in-house lawyers to partner with their clients, share the same goals and objectives and exercise as much business acumen as legal judgment.

Chapter 10: The evolving law department – what the future holds

By Patrick J Lamb, founder of ElevateNext Law and vice president of Elevate Services

No business *wants* to have a law department: businesses have law departments because they *must*. Of late, there has been much conversation about law departments evolving from a necessary evil, the department of "no," to valued part of the business. Even as some law firms are evolving in this manner, the pressure on corporate law departments is growing geometrically, perhaps exponentially. Change is happening faster than ever, and general counsel who are not keeping pace will be challenged to have a plan to do so and begin executing it sooner rather than later.

While change in business is accelerating, change in law departments – not to mention their law firms – is not happening anywhere near fast enough to keep up. Most CEOs are focused like a laser on digitizing their businesses, fundamentally transforming it. This is happening with incredible speed: 85 percent of business decision-makers see the transition happening in just two years, and fear financial jeopardy or losing ground to competitors if they cannot execute on this issue.[1] However, nearly 60 percent of these CEOs are concerned their businesses "do not have the sensory capabilities and innovative processes to respond to rapid disruption."[2] Businesses can ill-afford to have a law department that does not keep pace with the businesses they serve. It is unlikely CEOs will have patience with law departments that do not have a strategy for keeping up.

Think about that for a moment. Corporate law departments need to significantly accelerate their ongoing transformation *just to keep up with their businesses!* Few departments have developed their modernization plans, and fewer still are executing those plans. There are, however, a few "test lab" law departments that provide a glimpse into the future. Within the past year, Univar general counsel Jeffrey Carr announced his "moonshot" goal of reducing legal spend in his $8 billion chemical distribution company by 50 percent. A year ago, Microsoft announced it would be shifting away from the billable hour for most engagements. Both Carr and Microsoft's deputy general counsel, Neal Suggs, have spoken about creating new types of relationships to handle their respective company's legal needs. Their approaches are worth studying and emulating.

Understanding the role of the law department in a modern business

The present

The critical issue facing law departments is growing demand. As companies change, grow and globalize, the legal challenges grow. As technology rapidly advances, the gulf between business and law grows wider at an accelerating rate. Famed economist Herbert Stein once posited that "if something cannot go on forever, it will stop."[3] Law departments simply cannot continue without materially changing their approach.

Since they began, law departments served several functions, but the two most important were cleaning up messes made by business units and serving as the company's interface with law firms that were performing the company's legal work – sort of a cross between a janitorial service and a dating app. The economic pressures of the past decade forced law departments to reexamine their relationships with their outside counsel and make more informed "make v. buy" decisions. These decisions resulted in law departments expanding and bringing in significant amounts of work to be done by lower-priced in-house lawyers, to the detriment of outside firms. But little was done to address the "janitorial service" nature of law department workload, and now the perception is generally that little of the remaining work done by outside counsel can be economically moved inside. The challenge corporate law departments now face boils down to the simple matter of supply and demand: the demand for legal resources continues to grow rapidly, but the supply of internal resources is not rising correspondingly; the labor arbitrage model of shifting work from expensive resources to less expensive resources has largely run its course or is, at best, a short-term solution.

Modern law departments – the ones that intend to keep up with their businesses – will challenge the conventional wisdom and develop strategies and practices which defy the fundamental rules of supply and demand that relate to departmental operation.

The future – an overview

The next generation of law departments will have five essential components. First, to address the "janitorial" problem – cleaning up after problems created by the operation of the company – the legal department will embed lawyers in each of the business units in sufficient number to help critical decision-makers make better decisions. What's a better decision? One that makes the business unit successful and reduces demand on the law department.

Second, the law department will become disciplined at requiring other parts of the business to perform the operations they need to instead of letting those business units transfer their work to the law department. An example of this is contract drafting and negotiation. Most companies have sales personnel secure agreement on price, quantity and delivery date, and then toss the matter to the law department to formalize into a contract. While the law department should own the contracting process, the operational, technical and financial aspects of the corporation must own their respective components of the contract. For example, a contract to sell a product that must operate deep in the ocean has commercial, technical, financial and legal components. The commercial and technical departments are in the best position to know whether the company can perform, and the finance or accounting department is in the best position to know whether it can do so profitably. The legal department addresses the risk to the company if it fails to perform.

Third, the company will also employ modernized process development. Most tasks performed by the legal department have been done before, but nevertheless will involve time and energy to figure out how to do them again. Developing refined processes, supported by checklists, saves time and ensures consistency and quality in the service delivered. The future involves creating those processes and checklists.

Fourth, successful law departments will focus relentlessly on prevention. To that end, various data analytics will play a significant role. Analytics will provide insight into risks created by acquisition, foreign operations, and even employee performance variations. It will involve more mundane data such as quantifying the amount of time lawyers spend on various tasks – for example, some departments spend considerable time answering questions about contract meaning or about credit and bankruptcy issues. The data gathered about this issue will help general counsel allocate resources that can be used to reduce those areas of demand.

Finally, the modern law department will fundamentally change its relationship with its legal vendors, both law companies and law firms. Without fundamental change, law firms and companies will not make the investments needed to develop the technology the legal department needs – there will be no economic incentive to do so. And because few law departments have the resources to develop the necessary tech, they will not be capable of self-funding. A major Catch 22. As a result, the nature of the relationships will have to change from a series of simple transactions – "handle this matter" – to something far more collaborative.

The future – a more detailed look

Changing law departments is hard work. Damned hard. The same goes for changing law firms and law companies. No one who decides they need to be ready for the future should embark on the journey expecting smooth sailing. Indeed, expect the opposite – a bumpy ride, complete with setbacks along the way. But believe in the vision and learn from those who have started building this road before you.

1. Embedding lawyers in business units

One of the advantages in-house lawyers have over outside counsel is that in-house lawyers know more about the company's business. However, when one digs deeper, we learn that while this relative advantage is true, the depth of in-house counsel's knowledge is often not as comprehensive as it could be. In-house counsel may not be at key business meetings for operating parts of the business; they may not have a high level of familiarity with products, methods of operations, procedures and policies, strategies, research and development, financial issues, and so much more.

In an ideal world, there should be a "business unit lawyer attached to hip of the unit president or other chief officer," and the lawyer would be so plugged in "he or she would have a tissue ready to hand the business unit leader before she knew she was going to sneeze," according to Jeff Carr. True immersion maximizes the opportunities to shape events and decisions in ways which prevent legal problems from ever arising.

The relationships created with day-to-day decision makers will increase the likelihood of the in-house lawyer being consulted regarding decisions that, without guidance, might turn problematic. The best legal problems are the ones that are avoided, of course. Embedding lawyers deeply into business units therefore helps the law department reduce demand by reducing the number of business matters that evolve into legal problems.

2. Requiring business units to assume responsibility for their own work

Because lawyers tend to be problem-solvers, they tend to try to do so for other people. The other people are thrilled to be rid of the problem. In his best-selling book *The One Minute Manager Meets the Monkey*, author Kenneth Blanchard uses this example:

> In the hallway, an employee raises a problem with the boss. The boss shows some interest in the problem, and quickly the brief discussion has become a 20-minute session, which is abruptly ended when the boss has to attend a planned meeting. The discussion ends with the boss saying, "I don't have any more time now; let me think about it and I'll get back to you."

The boss has taken the employee's problem – the monkey on his back – and made it his own. The employee has one less problem to deal with, and the boss has one more. Substitute "lawyer" for "boss", and you see the problem.

Contract review is a classic example. Many business contracts involve agreements to buy and sell goods or services. The contracting company's ability to sell a particular good or service is not a legal issue – it is a business issue. If there is a question about the company's technical ability to make a particular product, the company has both a business issue and a technical one. And the issue of whether a price is enough to earn a profit is most certainly not a legal issue. It is the business' monkey. However, in most companies, the monkey – the drafting and review of contracts, with redlines going back and forth with the other contracting party – is taken away from the business and put on the back of the company lawyers. And they willingly take the monkey!

If you start with the goal of only being responsible for legal portions of the contract, you have substantially less work to do. What are legal portions of the contract? Pretty simple really – what happens if the company fails to perform the contract or the other side fails to perform its obligations? Disputes. And within disputes is the subcategory of indemnity risk – what kind of damages might the company be liable for? Many companies have firm positions that they will not accept the risk of consequential damages, or that such damages are capped by the amount of the contract. Regardless of position, that issue is most certainly a legal one.

So why does the monkey typically end up on a lawyer's back? Conventional wisdom is that a contract is a legal document, so therefore a lawyer must write it. Does that analysis hold up? Not at all. An expense report is a financial document, but employees fill out their own expense reports. The accounting and finance department most certainly does not fill out those forms. And thus lawyers have to learn the difference between owning a process and serving as operator. It makes sense for the law department to own the contracting process. That would include what parts of the document are essential; what parts allow for small or large modifications; what approvals are required for deviations from approved language; and, of course, provisions regarding disputes and risk.

Does this business empowerment approach work? Let me start from the standpoint of my experience of having litigated contract disputes for 35 years. More often than not, the business people on one side or both would have little or no informed understanding of what was agreed to – they were strangers to the document. The lawyers often were long gone but the legalese remained, as did the ambiguity occasioned by the fact that the provisions were drafted by lawyers, not the people who would be operating the process that was the subject of the contract. Strike one. Strike two is that contracts are often thrust upon those expected to perform them without any regard for whether the company can actually do so. This happens because the sales personnel are paid based on sales closed, and the operations group only gets the monkey put on its back after the contract is finalized, not when it has the ability to say, "hey, we can't do X and this price" or offer other pushback to ensure the contract makes sense operationally. Strike three is often the bottleneck created by legal review. The review of legal issues can be accomplished in minutes, but the legal review of the rest of contract takes much longer because the lawyers have to learn what the parties actually agreed to and then agree with other strangers to the deal (the other company's lawyers) as to what was agreed upon. Contract velocity – which translates into revenue velocity – can be enhanced by making those responsible for various portions of the contract own the monkey associated with that section.

This type of change to the contract review system challenges companies because people despise change and no one wants their monkey given back to them. The legal team will therefore face change management issues, but the outcome is a significant reduction of demand, both from a better contracting process and from reducing the number of disputes arising from executed contracts.

3. Process development

Process has a bad reputation among lawyers. Lawyers tend to view what they do as "special" and "bespoke," or otherwise customized. Lawyers fear being identified as purveyors of a commodity product. The problem with this line of thinking is that most legal work is the execution of process. Sometimes the process leads to the application of judgment, but oftentimes the execution of the process yields the end result. And every company has processes it must follow. Standardizing work squeezes fat out of the operation, allows for consistent quality, and – in many cases – enables the execution of needed work via application of tech or lower-cost resources.

The key to process development is identifying the steps that must be done and the order in which the steps must be accomplished. An automotive assembly line does not start with the installation of doors. The sequence is important. So is requiring everyone to do the same tasks the same way. If people are free to change the manner they do certain tasks, there is no longer a process, just a suggestion. This is where most law firms struggle – partners are autonomous, after all – and where law companies excel.

Process development is a tough, complex subject that I will not attempt to teach here. Instead, I want to highlight some examples to illustrate the importance of process. Consider an area like trademarks. Most companies have them, and they need to be managed. However, for most companies, there are not so many that you need a full-time inside resource devoted to trademarks. You can hire an outside lawyer to handle all of the work, but at considerable expense; alternatively, you can create detailed processes that a paralegal can execute, consulting a specialized trademark lawyer only when required.

Even an area as random as litigation can be "processified." The right steps, taken in the right order, can assure that insurance assets are fully utilized; that cases are always assessed early and based on the same protocol; and that the risk posed by a case is measured on a consistent basis so the resources allocated to it are proportional. Even something as small as the sequence in which discovery is analyzed can produce risk – the effort to respond is measured and then set against the validity of objections. Only valid objections that relate to a significant effort or risk are pursued; discovery motions are generally lost and are frequently expensive. Most of the time, the expense is unwarranted and could have been avoided.

There is process work to be done in every area of corporate law department practice. A lawyer should never have to figure out from scratch how to do something that he or she has done before, or that someone else in the law department has done previously. Effort should be put into a process and the process should then be shared. The cost savings associated with effective process development is significant.

4. Prevention, prevention, prevention

The law department of the future must reduce the demand for its services, or at a minimum reduce the rate of the demand growth. If growth is not curbed, demand will outstrip resources, putting the law department's essential mission at risk. Some law departments are already experiencing the phenomenon. For most others, it is just a matter of time.

The most effective tool to achieve this goal – prevention – ironically is considered suspect simply because it is hard to measure the value of avoided risk. That concern, however valid, is a poor reason not to implement an aggressive approach to prevention. Consider fire prevention as an analogy. We consider fire-fighters to be heroes, yet every single fire-fighter will urge prevention. The best fire, like the best legal problem, is the one that never happens. In this context, we require smoke alarms in homes; we post fire risk warnings in forests and national parks; and we ban campfires. It is hard to know exactly how many fires are avoided or lives saved by these measures, but we know they are successful. And so, after many years, we continue to utilize these safety measures and employ new prevention ideas when they emerge.

Consideration of a prevention strategy immediately begs the question of what is involved. The execution of a prevention strategy requires a prevention mentality. Few lawyers have this mentality innately; it is a learned behavior. As such, it requires practice regularly enough to become a habit. Because the demands of daily responsibilities tend to prevent the development of new habits, someone needs to be made responsible for implementing the processes and procedures which will give life to a prevention mentality throughout the department, and eventually throughout the business units as well.

Among the tactics a prevention specialist will utilize are root cause analyses on every problem, including litigation, to determine how to avoid them and using the outcomes to create new processes or procedures to avoid their repetition. The prevention specialist also will act as a quality assurance person, ensuring that processes and procedures are followed rigorously. There is more, but this should be sufficient to get the ball rolling.

5. Refining relationships with service partners

Most law departments only have relationships with law firms. That is changing, as more law departments have established relationships with law companies. Among other things, law companies execute the process development discussed in point three above much more capably than law firms. Law companies thrive on developing repeatable processes and then using personnel who did not attend law school and are much less expensive to accomplish the processified work. Law firms tend to eschew this approach because each partner is essentially autonomous, able to do things their own way. Every matter is handled as a unique, stand-alone phenomenon. This approach fails to extract the fat that can be removed by careful processes.

Microsoft – though its move away from hourly billing – has learned that hourly billing interferes with the immersion into the company's business that is needed to create new value. Microsoft deputy general counsel Neal Suggs described the hourly billing problem this way:

> *In the past, outside lawyers did their best to understand our business, but there was no way they could get the depth of knowledge they would derive from being immersed in it every day. Immersion wasn't an option – the hourly billing model prevented it – so outside counsel delivered legal advice, and inside lawyers had to take the time and effort to figure out how it applied to their businesses.*
>
> *Businesses can't operate that way anymore. Our industry changes too quickly, our business grows at an ever-expanding rate, and the law is too far behind. We not only need reliable legal advice fast, but we also need it to come to us in a way that's already tailored to fit very particular business contexts.*[4]

The result has been a huge win for both Microsoft and its commercial firm, Perkins Coie:

> *The first year under the new model was a win for Microsoft and Perkins Coie alike. Perkins Coie hit their goals and received their performance bonus. More importantly, though, the firm's attorneys clearly became more engaged with Microsoft's business. Unshackled from the desire to limit billable hours, the Microsoft team is no longer discouraged from looping in outside counsel for calls, meetings and other opportunities to help them learn the nuances of Microsoft's business. The Perkins Coie attorneys have started delivering legal advice that reflects those nuances and considers the company's needs and goals in ways you wouldn't usually see from an outside firm.*
>
> *Microsoft gets access to Perkins Coie's deep bench of experts and their broad range of experience, which complement the internal team's deep knowledge of its technology and business. All this makes the Microsoft commercial legal group a more valuable contributor to the law department and to the entire enterprise. The result is a relationship that not only serves Microsoft's legal needs but also helps build value for the business.*[5]

Univar has experienced a similar result. The Elevate and ElevateNext personnel working for Univar have learned the nuances of both the law department and the business units in ways that help us better advise and serve the customer. Without a non-hourly fee arrangement, this immersion and application of the resulting insight would not have been possible.

In addition to better service, both Microsoft and Univar are benefitting from work done by their teammates, Perkins Coie and Elevate, to design technology tools which facilitate even better service and greater insight to the customer into the work being performed by all members of the law department's teammates.

Having been serving clients using non-hourly billing arrangements for more than a decade, I know first-hand that the outcomes experienced by Microsoft and Univar are predictable, not serendipitous. Elevate's experiences with several of its customers confirms the belief that immersion and alignment of economic interests produces powerfully positive results.

Conclusion

Law departments cannot continue as they are in the face of the ever-growing demand for their services. The changes of the past decade have allowed departments to successfully keep pace with the changes in their business, but as change accelerates even more, new strategies and approaches will be necessary. Microsoft and Univar have taken steps that appear to be a productive way to position their law departments for success in the face of this accelerating pace of change in their quite disparate industries. The work has revealed the essentials of a workable strategy for success.

References

1. https://www.microstrategy.com/us/resources/blog/bi-trends/17-statistics-showcasing-the-role-of-data-in-digital-transformation
2. https://advisory.kpmg.us/articles/2017/destination-unknown.html
3. http://www.aei.org/wp-content/uploads/2013/06/-130606-media-steins-law_094731626218.pdf
4. https://www.law.com/corpcounsel/2018/12/17/beyond-the-billable-hour-its-not-about-economics-its-about-relationships/
5. Id.